GERALDINE BROOKS

May 27, 2019
West Tisbury

"Is Tony Horwitz living here?"
Yes, "To whom am I speaking?"
His wife is this.
It's exactly that. The remainder is a haze.
"Tried to resuscitate him at the scene after he collapsed in the street, but was taken to the hospital without success."
He is currently in the operating room. He is currently being hospitalized. We are currently holding him for observation.
There were many things that made sense.
However, she doesn't say any of these things. Rather, the nonsensical thing:
He is no longer alive.
No.
Not Tony. Not him. Not my spouse traveling the world fervently to promote his latest book. My spouse has the toned physique of someone who works out six days a week. When I first met him in his twenties, he was sixty years old and still wore clothing that was the same size. My husband, younger than I am—funny, full of energy. He lives a busy life. He can't be dead.
The resident's voice is worn and flat. When I ask her to repeat what she just said, she becomes irritated with me. She informs me that her shift is coming to a close. She provides me with the phone number of the physician who will be on duty in this emergency room located in Washington, D.C., five hundred miles away. She is unable to put me off the phone quickly enough.
However, I must visit Tony. When I arrive, where will he be? "A body cannot be kept in the emergency room." It will be taken to the hospital morgue so the DC medical examiner can get it.
It. A corpse. She's referring to Tony.

How will I see him, then? I'm on an island in Massachusetts. She interrupts, "It will take me hours to get there."

"You will need to speak with the DC police. Verify that they can get to you.

Then she disappears.

In the middle of this call, I got up from my desk. After being distracted all morning, I had just set down to work when the phone rang at eighteen minutes past one. On the phone, I had a pleasant chat with my oldest son, a recent college graduate who was traveling the world and getting ready to board an aircraft in Manila for the eight-hour journey to Sydney, where he would stay with my sister. An acquaintance named Susanna had come to return or borrow a book, but I can't remember which one. After delivering hay to the horses, we stayed out in the paddock, chatting while draping on the split rails.

Tony had sent me a lengthy email the day before, detailing his visit to the Virginia community where we had spent ten years. It caught me up on the activities of our former neighbors, including their struggles with dry wells and divorces ("she refers to him as her was-band"), and was largely unpunctuated and gossipy. "I didn't wish myself back there (if for no other reason, 90 degrees and 100 percent humidity, and still May), but I'm encouraged that it seems to have subtly changed while preserving its history and quirk," the email said. I'm going back to work tomorrow, and since I'm already two or three episodes behind on Billions, you'll need to watch it again when you get back. Hugs and affection

I sent my response and then opened the file called Horse, which was the novel I was meant to write.

Next, the telephone.

An additional diversion. I contemplated leaving it on voicemail.

Perhaps, however, my older son had overlooked a question. My younger son was away at boarding school taking his final exams for the year. He might have needed something. I had to pick it up.

In the intense sunlight, it was difficult to discern the caller ID. GW HSP was only visible on the screen when I drew the phone closer. Tell me I didn't answer a fucking fundraising call.

The tone on the dial burned now. I looked at the phone. I felt my legs tremble. But I was unable to sit. As I walked the room, I could feel the howl growing within me. I felt like screaming, crying, hurling myself on the ground, ripping my clothes, and tearing my hair.

I couldn't let myself do any of those things, though.

as there were a lot of other things I needed to do.

That roar was stifled as I stood there. since I was on my own and nobody could assist me. I might also be unable to get back up if I let go and fall.

No one learns this information alone in novels or films. A visitor approaches the door. After making sure you're seated, someone offers you water and asks who they should call.

However, nobody had shown me such generosity. After picking up my husband's cell phone—which he had never set up a passcode on—a weary young doctor pressed the fast dial for "Home."

The first harshness I would discover is that the system is cruel and flawed.

February 2023
Essendon

The little prop plane departs from Essendon Airport in Melbourne. Container terminals, suburban rooftops, and the Yarra River's industrialized mouth. The image I had hoped for—the sparkling, island-studded Bass Strait—is then blocked when we break through a flat layer of clouds. I can only gaze at the propeller's captivating blur. Concentric circles in a smear. Flight's unlikely physics.

To complete the unfinished task of grieving, I'm going to a cabin on the farthest end of Flinders Island. I now understand that the actions I took on that day in late May 2019 and the obligations I had to fulfill in the days and months that followed had cost me an unseen price. To pay for it, I'm traveling to this isolated island.

I hear brief snippets of speech from my fellow passengers within the little aircraft, such as, "I've got a hundred acres, it's quite a big bit of dirt."

"Since we were there last year, nobody has probably fished that location."

"If you're building a place, you have to take the cell tower into consideration, even if you have the views and bars."

"There are no pins left."

"Gone, what do you mean?"

"Gone, buddy," I mean. Not present.

Tony died on Memorial Day, the American holiday commemorating the war dead that falls on the final Monday in May.

I'll start my own memorial days as soon as I arrive at Flinders Island. The right to grieve is something that our culture no longer freely grants. block external demands. to sense the depth of his loss and to remember my affection. In his book The Smell of Rain on Dust, Martín Prechtel writes, "Grief is praise because it is the natural way love honors what it misses."

I haven't given Tony the respect he deserves because I haven't given myself the time and space to grieve deeply enough to capture our love. I will finally be able to meet people without having to prepare a face for them. the location where I won't have to act like everything is fine and that I'm alright. Because, despite appearances, I am not at all okay, and it has been over three years. Since Tony's passing, I've come to see that my life has been one long, draining act. I have positioned myself as a typical woman. I've walked about in public enacting a number of plausible roles, such as author on tour, conservation commissioner, and PTO mother. However, nothing has been typical. The long-running show finally takes a break at this point.

The Hebrew scriptures' small passageway, the maytzar, has imprisoned me. The singer in the Psalms calls out to God from a small space, and God responds from his "wideness." The Hebrew word maytzar and our English word "anguish" have the same meaning. It comes from the Latin word constraint, straitness, and narrowness. The great breadth of a complex, florid, demonstrative sadness is something I have not permitted myself. Rather, there has been a persistent sensation of restriction, of suppressing and stifling it so that it does not manifest.

I don't practice deism. My prayers will go unanswered. I find the wideness I'm looking for in time, in nature, and in silence.

And I have purposefully chosen this island, this location. My life had started to lead me here before I met Tony. My life was completely turned upside down when I fell in love with him. I might now get a peek of what I've been missing, take that unexplored path, and reflect on the person I could have become.

Perhaps I will be able to escape the matter at last, alone on this island at the end of the world. However, I must first return to that time in my brightly illuminated study when I forbid myself from howling. In my heart's basement, that howl has turned into a beast. I must figure out how to publish it.

May 27, 2019
West Tisbury

"You will need to speak with the DC police. Verify that they can get to you.
I had to wait for that call by the landline, though, because she hadn't asked for my cell phone and I hadn't provided it to her. In between, I looked for my phone, which I hardly ever used back then, and started working on the tasks at hand.
I called the airport first. I know the people who staff the desks by name at this little, rural airport. Are they able to remove me from the island? Could there be a seat?
Not on Memorial Day weekend. Summer officially begins this long weekend. Months had gone into booking every flight departing Martha's Vineyard that afternoon.
After taking the ferry to the mainland, I would need to drive three hours to Boston in the hopes of catching a flight to Washington, DC. At 2:30 p.m., the next ferry was scheduled to arrive. If I parked the car in an unauthorized area, I might be able to make it.
The home phone then rang. Evelyn, a DC police detective. He was kind and thoughtful. After the harsh doctor, I was grateful for this unexpected act of goodwill. He told me that Tony had been strolling in that very spot when he collapsed, and that a former Vietnam doctor was the first to notice him laying on the ground. As he examined Tony's vital signs, he asked someone to call 911. Because Tony had fainted directly on the line between the District of Columbia and the Maryland suburbs, the investigator explained, two ambulances—one from Chevy Chase and one from Washington, DC—arrived within minutes after women from the yoga studio across the street ran out with a defibrillator. The detective did not know how long either of the EMT teams had been working on him before sending him to the downtown emergency room.

He questioned me about Tony's health and the reason for his visit to Washington, DC. He clarified that an autopsy would be required to rule out foul play because no witnesses were present when he collapsed. I asked the man who had located Tony if I could talk to him. He promised to try to connect me with someone. I gave him my cell number and informed him that I was heading to the ferry.

I then searched for Tony's brother Josh's phone number. He had traveled to Maine with the other members of the Horwitz family to attend his daughter's college graduation. Little mercies: Tony's mother, Ellie, was present. When she got this unimaginable news, supportive and caring people would surround her.

Tony had been residing in Josh's vacant Chevy Chase home. He had been on a strict schedule since the release of his book, but the Memorial Day holiday weekend had provided a much-needed respite. He had traveled the entire country and completed eight events in seven days. He was always so tired from getting up early for flights, staying late at book signings, and then going out for drinks with the old pals who always showed up at those events, according to all of his emails. He called me to tell me how nice it felt to have some rest after sleeping for hours when he finally arrived at his brother's house. Feeling rejuvenated by Sunday afternoon, he had traveled to see our former friends in Waterford, the small community of around 80 families in the Blue Ridge foothills where we had spent ten years. All he needed to do was attend a meal with friends from Washington in his honor on that slow Memorial Day Monday. He would resume his tour the following day. He had numerous interviews scheduled beginning early in the morning, followed that evening by a book event at Politics and Prose, the renowned bookstore in Washington, DC.

However, the next day did not exist.

"Northampton Street?" When I told Josh where Tony had fallen, he mumbled in shock. "My house is only a block away from that."

Tony's older brother, Josh, had grown from a mischievous young man to the family's pillar of support and the person you wanted in an emergency. He promised to immediately find a flight from Maine.

Ellie would be driven to Washington, DC, by his sister Erica and her husband David. The two young ladies had to return to their professions and schools, so his wife, Ericka, would take their daughters to their different planes. He predicted that he would probably get to his residence before me. He could hear the fear in my voice. Think about what you should pack for a moment. You may stay for a while.

I disregarded his advice and left the house wearing what I planned to wear for the next three days. I was only able to think of a toothbrush and some underwear. To secure the final seat on the flight I had reserved to Washington, DC, I had to take the two-thirty ferry. I called Fred and Jeanne, my neighbors, to let them know what had happened and ask if they could watch the horses and our dogs. They will, without a doubt. They will immediately approach.

The first doctor had given me the number of the resident who had relieved her for the evening shift, and I called it while on the boat. This young man had no idea what I was talking about or who I was. He was obviously overburdened by other people's crises.

"How should I know?" he yelled at me when I inquired about whether Tony's body would still be at the hospital when I arrived.

I'm not sure why, but I had higher expectations than this.

Do no harm first.

Flinders Island

A burst of wind grabs my hat as soon as I get off the plane. I managed to grab it in time. This island—this beautiful, eerie island—lies squarely in the path of the Roaring Forties, which are winds that blow westerly at this latitude without being blocked by any continent. These winds are brought down from the equator toward the South Pole. The midday light feels warm against my face in February, late summer. However, the wind is strong enough to ruin your tea.

Only once, while researching a book that touched on the island's tragic past but which I never published, did I visit this place with Tony.

Both of us were awed by this island's splendor and adored it. I enjoyed it more than he did, though, as with everything related to Australia. Although I was able to get Tony to spend some time in Sydney during our marriage, I was unable to convert him to Australian culture since he was fundamentally American. He never developed the same appreciation for the nation that I do, despite my expectations, hopes, and longings for him to have a different perspective. "A gorgeously civilized land next to America but at the same time smug and sun-struck...not a place I want to live, something I can't even discuss with G. without her becoming tearful or angry," he wrote in his notebook in 1994, ten years after we were married.

It was one of the few topics we disagreed on, and I lost the argument. Compromise is a constant in marriage. Tony was the one who gave in on many crucial issues. He followed me to Cleveland, Sydney, and Cairo, molding his career around mine for years. On this most basic matter, however, he won. I never came to terms with it.

Like newborn goslings, we leave our mark on a certain kind of horizon. When a reporter asked Barbara Kingsolver what she liked best about Appalachia, she replied, "On a type of sky." My pellucid sky holds the Southern Cross; my imprinted horizon is the Pacific Ocean, surrounded by sinuous gum trees and rocky headlands. For me, though, it's more than just landscape. It is also a national celebrity. An easygoing, self-deprecating way of going about the world with a smile on your face and a hand ready to be thrown back to assist your lagging companion. a national consensus that prioritizes the welfare of the masses over personal preferences.

He depended on his nation, but we all adored ours. It served as his inspiration. It fueled the work he was passionate about. He did it with remarkable foresight, intelligence, and wit, connecting the past and present of America. My job can be done anyplace and is primarily done in my own mind. To raise my sons in a nation whose beliefs and decisions frequently felt incomprehensible, I accepted an expatriation that I did not want. I believe there is a considerable probability that I would have ended up on Flinders Island rather than Martha's Vineyard, where we would have ultimately established ourselves after years of traveling the world as foreign correspondents, if I had never met Tony and had never loved him with fervent devotion. The careless shimmer of water that you unexpectedly discover when you turn a corner or climb a hill was a typical feature of most of the areas we decided to dwell in. Our first houses together were on Sydney's Balmain Peninsula, followed by an island in the Nile in Egypt, then Martha's Vineyard, an island eight miles off the coast of Massachusetts, where we eventually made our home and reared our children. We spent over half our married life there.

Examining the price of my compromise is one of the reasons I have decided to attend these memorial days at Flinders rather than some remote location. What would my life have been like if I had actually chosen this beautiful island as the destination of my untraveled path, raising Australian children and penning Australian novels? What would you have lost and what would you have gained? I can't truly address these questions, but they still bother me. The prerequisite, if not the sufficient, condition for considering this more clearly than my hazy old memories of the location permit is to return here.

I sign for a rental car inside the little airport terminal on Flinders Island, which the young woman at the desk warns me "has some damage." Black pen marks on the vehicle's schematic on the papers

indicate dings on nearly every panel. You can easily identify it; it's the one with the front bumper that has been torn in two and repaired with Steri-Strips' counterpart for cars. These are the customs of a far-flung rural location where practically everything you need is delivered on a Wednesday by barge. I think this is fantastic; it's very Australian. I can't stop listening to John Williamson's anthem, "True Blue":
Will you tie it up with wire,
just to keep the show on the road?
Getting food is the first thing I do. The closest supermarket is about thirty miles away from the shack I'm renting, and half of that distance is on a rough dirt road that is impassable above ten miles per hour from sunset to sunrise if you don't want to kill the local nocturnal fauna, which includes wallabies, pademelons, and wombats.
As is customary in this small town, the woman who gives me the provisions also works for the shack's owner, so I get directions: "Turn right back up by the airport and just keep going." It's unlocked. "We lack Nothing." A location like mine. Our house on the Vineyard, built in the 1740s, had no locks on the doors when we purchased it.
I see what is similar to and different from the Vineyard as I travel north along the island's west shore. Beaches encircle both islands; some are wide and sandy, while others are small and cove-like. The Vineyard's year-round population is perhaps fifteen times that of Flinders Island, and it is further boosted by the summer flood of visitors and second-home owners. Nevertheless, both islands feature acres of pristine forests and marshes and expansive stretches of farmland that sweep toward the coast. Although many of the Vineyard's humble dwellings have been razed in favor of opulent summer complexes that are out of proportion to island custom, the residences are comparable in certain ways—they are farmsteads and beach cottages.
The geology is where the differences are most apparent. The Vineyard is a terminal moraine, which is made up of low hills of stones and clay soils that an old glacier drove out into the ocean. The island chain that includes Flinders is the remains of a land bridge that was formerly used to connect Tasmania with the Australian mainland. At either

extremity of the island, two towering peaks, one to the north and one to the south, push into the sky like exclamations, encircling a stony mountain spine.

I can tell I'm getting close to my destination as Mount Killiecrankie, the northern peak, comes into view. I bump down the steep route to the shack after turning off the main road.

Here, in this lovely place, I am alone. Already eager and impatient for the first excursion, Tony should be there, carrying the wheelie bag. I suddenly remember him clearly from our recent trip to Tasmania. He had made the decision to use the trip to kick his nicotine gum addiction, and when we were unable to find the hotel room we had reserved right away, he stomped his foot and sat down on his wheelie bag, looking as cranky and obnoxious as a toddler. I had told him to go get some Nicorette after the lads and I had laughed at him.

That memory makes me grin. We took the boys back to Sydney towards the end of that trip, and we spent our thirtieth wedding anniversary together on a secluded beach on Tasmania's east coast.

Now, I'm the only one pushing the wheelie bag across the uneven terrain. I accept and allow sadness to arise. This is the current situation. lonely.

But directly behind that, a boisterous inner voice is asking, "What's up with you?" and yapping like an unruly terrier. You're fortunate to have the time and resources to accomplish this. And look at that landscape! The shack is made of mismatched wood and has only three basic rooms. It faces Mount Killiecrankie, a powerful granite swell that rises out of the ocean, and is situated at the southern end of a deep, goblet-shaped bay. Vibrant Caloplaca, a symbiotic relationship between algae and fungi, paints the boulders in tangerine-colored streaks. I stand there in awe of the orange rock's magnificence and the water's many shades of blue, which are as brilliant and changing as the hues of peacocks' feathers.

After putting the food in the tiny refrigerator, I went for a stroll down the shore. It turns out that this hike is more difficult than it appears. Its steep bend hides its actual length. It is two p.m. when I leave the shack.

When I return, it's four thirty. The beach is broad and vast during low tide, and the beautiful white sand feels sturdy underfoot. The other person is the only one. A woman tosses a ball to her dog as they play in the distance. As I approach, I can see that the dog is white and ginger, resembling a Brittany spaniel. Since the beach is so large, altering my course would seem rude. I pass them without intruding. I turn to see that they have disappeared up some invisible path among the dunes, leaving me alone. I sense the remarkable nature of that. These miles of high dunes are a bit of a wonder—a globally uncommon example of natural coastal health—because most beaches this lovely have been built. My shanty is one of only a few modest buildings that are limited to a tiny section of the beach's rocky southern edge.

Eventually, the sand is replaced by rock shelves and pools as the dunes give way to granite that is upthrusting. Cuttlefish skeletons have been cracked. Some are a foot long and have been worn smooth by the wind to approximate topographical model features. I notice a gleaming curve that resembles a draftsman's spline. It is the ideal abalone shell's edge. It sparkles in vivid pinks and greens and ripples when I lift it out of the sand.

I want to tell Tony all this. I want him here by my side, to cuddle up on the deck and hold my hand into the late twilight, to feel the sting of the wind, to watch the moon rise above Mount Killiecrankie, shining as bright as a pearl.

Many of my friends are happily married. Ours is a long one. As fortunate as we were. They are in their sixties, have money and time to appreciate each other, have raised their children, and have done wonderful jobs, usually in the media or the arts. When they share their beautiful photos of themselves exploring Kakadu, paddling the Okavango, enjoying coffee in a Siena square, or stumbling into a lava field in Hawaii, I'm thrilled for them. I'm jealous, too.

After our younger son begged us to allow him to attend the boarding school that had recruited him for lacrosse, Tony and I were empty nesters for a little less than two years. I regretted his decision to go. I liked being a mother, even if I arrived late. I didn't want to be cheated out of four more years of working a day job. I also had doubts about prestigious private schools and their wealthy offspring. However, Bizu had desire and talent. To obstruct him looked churlish.

With only ourselves to think about, it ended up being a beautiful moment for the two of us. We could go out on the spur of the moment to a movie or restaurant rather than dragging ourselves along with schoolwork and sleeping for the first time in decades. We had a great trip to Oxford, where Tony was speaking about the debates over Civil War monuments and historical memory. We explored the golden stone's cobbled alleys, engaged in animated conversations in the taverns with low ceilings, and devised plans for returning for a longer stay.

What ambitious goals we had. After Tony's book was written, we would have a lot more adventures ahead of us.

Plans. Those, ah.

We all learned from COVID that planning is pointless. In case I hex myself, I've grown superstitious about the word. Never has the adage "make plans if you want to make God laugh" been more accurate. However, we would have started producing them now. Together.

I'm here instead. I'm missing him. By themselves.

May 27, 2019
Vineyard Haven Ferry

Make an effort to think. Make an effort to think. I had a hard time figuring out what I needed to do from the fog of intense emotion.

In Georgetown, there was Sally, who thought she would be entertaining Tony and ten of our friends for dinner in less than five hours. Sarah wove the complex web of his book tour, with its intertwining threads of interviews, appearances, and aircraft bookings, at Penguin Press and was now unfinished. And our longtime friend, Kris, our literary agent. She would be aware of any additional professional tasks that needed to be completed. And even as the boat horn rang and we backed away from the slip, I was supposed to be going to the Vineyard friends' party.

I would have known a lot of folks on this boat in the winter. The 45-minute drive across Vineyard Sound to Woods Hole on Cape Cod would have involved greetings, catch-ups, and talks. However, the boat was crowded with visitors near the end of the Memorial Day weekend. I was able to find a place to sit among strangers and avoid having to engage in conversations that I couldn't have.

The harbor's deep notch gives way to a broad strait of roaring currents, making for a stunning traverse. As the steamship moves between vibrant buoys that indicate safe passage across rocky shoals, gulls dive and hover above it. Tony and I had cherished and anticipated this crossing during our summer visits to the Vineyard. By putting a section of ocean between tension and leisure, the boat ride to the island signified the start of vacation in a concrete way. We would take a deep breath and release the tensions of the real world and work-related worries as we stood on the foredeck, holding hands and letting our hair blow in the sea wind. The trip back was a time of contentment, a chance to relish the moments we'd shared, the sweet conclusion to enjoyable moments.

However, I just wanted the crossing to end that day. I entered my information into my transportation app as we got closer to the mainland. As soon as we docked, I ran down the gangway to the waiting vehicle. When my buddy Susanna called, I had just secured my seat belt. The Vineyard is not very large. The grapevine had served its purpose. Someone had told someone at the airport. Now, the local paper's online version has published Tony's passing.

This was awful. I still hadn't gotten to our sons. This information would be kept from Nathaniel, the person traveling to Sydney, for a few more hours. How much I wanted to keep them both safe. Bizu was a sophomore in high school and only sixteen. In two and a half days, he would be out of school. He is our adoptive son, and at the age of five, he had already lived through all the losses of a lifetime. I told Susanna about my insane desire to conceal this information from him until I could reach him and embrace him, to allow him to complete his academic year. "No," she firmly said. "You must inform him. Now. You are aware that they are constantly on their phones. Would you like him to view it on the internet?"

I gave his school's principal, Peter, a kind man, a call. He promised to take Bizu to his workplace and provide him a supportive environment. They would then give me another call so I could deliver the news. I shivered in the backseat of a stranger's automobile for the next few minutes, picturing my son's suffering. How would he feel if his adviser pulled him out of class and brought him to the principal's office? I imagined him pacing nervously through the well-kept grounds of that beautiful school, past flower beds sprinkling with springtime blossoms. His final moments before everything fell apart. When he was a baby, his birth father—a soldier in the Ethiopian army—had passed away. Bizu has only ever known Tony as a father. Tony had been carrying him about on his shoulders for nearly a year when we brought him home, small and malnourished. What could I possibly say to him?

On a dark, dark day, that call and the sound of my son's cries in a place too far away to reach out and embrace him brought a new level of darkness.

At the airport, I wandered in a stupor through the lengthy, well-known hallway of Logan Terminal C, where I knew every Hudson, Wolfgang Puck, and Cibo, and the rigmarole of check-in and TSA screening. The gate lounge was packed with vacationers, leaving no seat unoccupied. Detective Evelyn contacted me when I was waiting to board. The former medic who had contacted Tony initially, Mr. Ryan, had consented to talk to me. He was anticipating my phone call. I turned my face to the wall as I typed the number, finding the most secluded and silent spot I could—a corner tucked away behind a pillar.

He was lying prone on the sidewalk when I saw him, and initially I assumed he was searching beneath his car. Then his glasses caught my eye. His distance from them was a foot and a half. I knew there had to be a problem.

Mr. Ryan described how he had hurried over to take Tony's pulse, which was weak and erratic, and noticed that he was breathing heavily and convulsively. At the local yoga class, he yelled out to a woman to dial 911. No injuries were visible; the fall must have been mild; perhaps Tony had fallen to his knees before collapsing slowly forward. He had not tried to halt his fall or even realized he was falling, as evidenced by the fact that his arms were by his sides. They began CPR after Linda, the yoga instructor, hurried out with the defibrillator from the studio. Paramedics then took over, saying, "I believe it was less than five minutes."

An endotracheal tube was placed there or in the emergency room. Multiple IV lines were placed and multiple ECG pads were put there or in the emergency room. Someone had given Amiodarone, the last-resort medication for ventricular fibrillation,.

"They spent a solid thirty minutes at the scene working diligently and effectively. However, he had no pulse and was unconscious. He hesitated. The women were stroking his head from the yoga studio. They were incredibly loving. thoughtful and compassionate.

I rambled some thanks to him for accepting my call and for attempting to assist Tony because I was too upset to reply.

He said, "I had a sister." She passed away in her flat by herself. Not knowing what her final moments were like has been awful. I'm happy to share this with you.

Flinders Island

Even though it's so calm here, I can't sleep. I have purposefully placed myself in the same situation as I was on the worst day of my life. Finding every memory of that period and feeling the full extent of the sadness I had suppressed from myself is what I came here to do.

Around two in the morning, I rise and go for a walk outside beneath the nearly full moon. A herd of grazing wallabies occupy the garden. They ran away, pursued by the shadows of their own moons, and I feel sorry for disturbing them. I return to my bed with the intention of reading for a while. I've brought along a few novels. The Light of the World by Elizabeth Alexander and A Widow's Story by Joyce Carol Oates are two books that were given as gifts by well-meaning individuals and describe the terrible repercussions of losing a spouse. The Year of Magical Thinking, Joan Didion's memoir, was already in our possession. The cheaply bound, uncorrected proofs of upcoming novels that publishers provide to critics before the hardcover's release are a ragged gallery. That year, Tony served as a judge for the National Book Award's nonfiction division. Didion's book was the winner.

Judge Tony, apparently, is not to be thanked. Tony has written the following on the galley's first page:

Name & product dropping. Padded.

Although I had been hesitant to read the book, I now smile at Tony's cold rejection of this well-known memoir. He has highlighted every reference to celebrities and high-end products throughout the galley and annotated any parts of text that he feels are overly dramatic. A lot of marking is present.

However, after reading it, I am unable to concur with his contemptuous assessment. Didion's story resonates so strongly with mine. The lengthy marriage, the entwined professions, and the unexpected, bewildering loss. I want to tell him to give her some time.

Her acquaintances were famous, and she worked in the film industry. She is powerless to stop it.

I can't read for long because the bed lamp isn't very strong. However, I am confident that I will revisit this book, and I like Tony's derogatory scribbles. It seems to me that we are reading it together and debating it amicably.

This book marking was one of the few things that separated us. I handle myself carefully. I look for autographed copies and early printings. To maintain new hardbacks in perfect condition, I remove the dust jackets while I'm reading them. I would scrawl on a painting or purposefully gouge a scratch in an old table before I would write in a book. Tony, meanwhile, was the opposite. Pen in hand, he read, writing down his ideas everywhere. I am now happy with this. I can find out what he thought of a book if I pick it up that I haven't read yet.

I don't wake up till late after I eventually fall asleep. The sea is high and the morning is gloomy and windy. I don't really know how I'm going to spend my time here. I'll take a stroll and think, accepting whatever comfort nature has to offer. Everything that comes to mind regarding Tony's passing and its consequences will be documented. I'm going to give myself the time and space I need to reflect about our marriage and feel the feelings I've been holding inside.

Granola, which I never eat at home, is what I eat as I wait for the ebb tide. It is as chewy and tasteless as I recall, so I'm not sure why I ordered it in the supermarket store. To observe the abundant life in the tidal pools, I started off in the opposite direction of the trek I had taken yesterday, heading west around the rock shelf.

The enormous limpets have designer stripes in tones of milk, russet, and sienna. Shining mica sheets and a smooth, yellowstone incursion with a cube-shaped crystal that I subsequently discover is orthoclase, potassium feldspar, are present. Samphire, often known as sea asparagus, is the greatest crunchy, salty food found in the ocean. As I pass the headland, a fresh view opens up: a tall, forested bluff covered with casuarinas and eucalyptus, punctuated by a dagger-shaped inlet.

Rock-hopping the granite boulders is difficult. Even though the chasm isn't very big, I reconsider crossing it as I reach it. It's remote out here if I trip. There would be no one to take me away. Rather, I move inland and smell the bush, upsetting the wallabies once more.

Then I come to a heap of slash. Many trees have been felled here. There's a new road in. I go up the bluff after it. The walk is steep. Even while there are occasionally breathtaking views from rocky outcrops, the sheer number of dead trees and the devastation depresses me. Roads cause habitat fragmentation, invasive species routes, soil erosion, and watercourse silting. This shrub appears immaculate. No invasive species are visible. How quickly will this new road alter that, I wonder? My heart sinks as I realize where the route seems to be going. An enormous multi-building property is located well across the valley, which is still uncommon on this island. On the otherwise pristine mountainside, alone. The access road is this one. The fact that one large house should be permitted to do so much damage is absurd. Not too long ago, Martha's Vineyard was similar to Flinders. However, a lot of new mansions like that one have caused invasive species to put strain on native plants and animals. Too much stress is causing the ponds to become eutrophic.

I return down the hill when I get to the top, just before the road drops to cross the valley. I'm not going to do that again.

Et in Arcadia ego.

May 27, 2019
Washington, D.C.

On June 9, 1958, Tony was born at George Washington University Medical Center. On May 27, 2019, at 12:38 p.m., he was declared dead there. At that hospital, his father, Norman Horwitz, worked as a neurosurgical practitioner and instructor. Alec, his grandfather, worked as a surgeon.

Tony had returned home to die after reporting on two wars in the Persian Gulf, avoiding rifle fire during the Romanian revolution, hitchhiking across the Australian outback, following Captain James Cook's Pacific voyages from the Arctic Circle to the edge of the Antarctic ice shelf, and traveling the world as a foreign correspondent, covering stories from Sarajevo's sniper pits and boats under shelling in Beirut harbor. He had collapsed just a few blocks from the brown-shingle Victorian house in Chevy Chase where he was raised, and had been declared dead in the hospital where he was born.

On a Monday, he passed away. Statistically, the most common day for cardiac arrest deaths is that one. The risk of having a heart attack that day is 20 percent higher for men in particular. The precise reason is unknown.

I requested to see my husband's body at the hospital reception desk. On this public holiday, I was led to a door immediately off the ER waiting area, which was brimming with suffering. I heard brief excerpts of ominous conversations between triage staff and patients. A stressed-out employee scowled at me in a closet-sized workplace. "You're the third person to inquire." I found out that Bob and Elsa, Joel and Mary, and other close friends from the city had come here separately in the hopes of joining Tony for vigil. "Unfortunately, I must inform you of what I told them: nobody is permitted." He extended his hands. "We have irate people and gunshot casualties in Washington, DC." When he saw my face crumple, he trailed off. "Your spouse may not even be present at this moment. Perhaps the medical examiner has already picked up. It's best to give them a ring in the morning.

He gave me a plastic bag. I gazed at it with confusion.

"His impacts."

His phone, glasses, wallet, flip-flops, and a crumpled newspaper page. Blindly, I grabbed the chair behind me and fell into it.

"I apologize," I stammered. But ever since, I've just been having trouble getting here. and now... and you now claim that I am unable to see him. The man held up his hand. "Take as much time as you like." After a bit, he returned with a paper cup of water. I made an effort to gather myself for the second time that day. I had to get out of this man's office since I was taking up space. I wiped my eyes and suppressed the wail my body yearned for once again.

I went outside into the steamy evening in Washington, DC, and made my way to the loading dock by walking around the hospital. I didn't think Tony had been picked up by the city coroner. Not during a holiday. I felt a crazy need to enter covertly, take some scrubs, and locate the morgue.

Join him.

Tony would do such things. He bribed a dry cleaner to sell him a Saudi army uniform while working as a reporter during the first Gulf War (only Saudis submit their fatigues to be dry cleaned; only Tony saw this and took action). As the first wave of Kuwaiti troops recaptured their city, he was the first American reporter to reach the front lines while disguised as a soldier.

I stood there for a while, trying to find the strength to pull off this crazy deed. Behind me, traffic flowed; ambulances came and went in a cacophonous rush of whirring lights and blaring sirens.

I'm not Tony. I was unable to summon his courage. To get to Josh's house, I turned and called a cab.

Flinders Island

My American cellphone rings at midnight. How could that be? It's in airplane mode now. I'm not meant to be reachable by phone here. (Only a few people are aware of my Australian number, which my kids have for emergencies.) I fumble for a response in the dark.

My friend Jim, a comedy writer from Los Angeles, is calling to ask if I might read and provide suggestions on the draft of a romantic comedy he has written. He is unaware that I am attempting to grieve for my husband, who has been gone for over three years, on an island in the Bass Strait.

I don't want to hurt his feelings, and it's just too difficult to explain. I therefore say the simple thing: Send it, of course.

I end the call, imagining how Tony would find this huge disconnect amusing. I picture how happy he would be if he took this story and worked it into something to entertain our friends at a dinner party.

Tony made me laugh every day. It is what I miss most about him, more than his soft hands or his lilting speaking voice. He was able to spot ridiculousness, cut through pretense, and execute realistic jokes with unfathomable reality. Our family was taught to be wary of April 1st and to guard against elaborate scams that could include a newspaper article that was mocked up in flawless typeface and that gave me the scoop on a news story I had been working on, or a convincingly dramatized phone call from a contractor claiming that the kitchen renovations were not up to code and would need to be demolished. One year, Tony fashioned gory mannequin corpses for the front garden and then dressed up in matching ketchup-smeared rags to lie on the lawn himself. The elaborate horrors Tony created made our neighborhood kids love coming here for Halloween. His "dummy" would come alive and start yelling as the children approached along the walkway.

He could be intense when writing; he was a perfectionist, and anyone who bothered him would suffer the consequences. You would only receive a grumpy grumble. He worked in a light-filled room we had made out of a former cow barn, lined with books. Upstairs at our former house, I wrote in a study. Several times a day, I could hear him scurrying into the kitchen to quickly acquire coffee to keep going. During these missions, I made no effort to engage with him since I knew from experience that it would be an unsatisfying encounter—the single occasion this hypersocial being was antisocial.

Even after the boys no longer needed my afternoon hovering, I continued to write during the school day. I liked the routine. Around four o'clock, I would wrap up my job and begin preparing dinner. After five o'clock, I would glance up through the kitchen window and see Tony, with his closed laptop tucked under his arm, strolling down the well-traveled path from the barn. I'd know the good times were coming. We would resume our talk where we had left it once I opened the wine. There was a lively, humorous party vibe every night.

At the end of the day, I miss those giggles.

Bizu has an eye for the ridiculous and brutal comic timing, and there are times when he makes me laugh almost as much as Tony did. I want more, though, like a hungry person on a diet. I've come to rely on friends that make me laugh, like Jim in LA.

Jim's early call is a reminder of how difficult it is to block the outside world. I made an effort to do all the tasks, pay all the bills, and respond to all the emails before I left home. However, I was inundated with fresh busywork when I went on for the final time to post an Away message. For a May literary festival, which flights would I like to take? Because they require me to use a new gateway for my invoice, the money for an essay I prepared in December did not process. I had to go back and review my records when a tradesman I believed I had paid issued his charge again.

The same old morass: We waste our powers by acquiring and spending.

After taking care of the urgent issues, I post the "Away" notice. They'll all have to wait this time.

How that one phone call from Los Angeles got through is beyond me. The internet listing for this hut alerted me to the patchy wi-fi and extremely bad cell connection on this side of the island. That, in my

opinion, made the location ideal for its intended use. However, the national telecom had completed a significant overhaul by the time I arrived a few months later.
There is currently good coverage throughout the island.
A night of violence. Winds as loud as a train and lashing rain. The small wooden hut moans under the might of the storm, pounded together with repurposed metals, rescued timbers, and recycled doors. Here, rain is valuable. It is the only source of drinking water, and I go back to sleep as I picture this flood sluicing down the tin roof and filling the tank with that necessary resource.
I began working on the task for which I came here this morning. I launch my laptop and move the pointer back through my sent emails to May 27, 2019, the terrible day. Everything as usual, followed by the email I wrote to Sally in Georgetown.

Header: Terrible news.
Tony died. The hospital just called. Apparently a massive heart attack. I will be in touch when I know more.

I keep reading. How quickly the ripples of loss widened. How swift the first brokenhearted reactions of friends. From Frankie:

There's so much I want to say to you, but for now, just this: I will always think of Tony as I saw him last, golden and electric, backlit by the sunset at Lambert's Cove.

I read this and I want to stop. But I make myself keep going, accepting the tightness in my chest, the radiating pain from my gut.
And as I read on, I see how quickly I fell into what would become my rote response to condolences.

We were so lucky.

It was there. Tony is not three hours dead, and my defense shield is already in place.

I have landed in the gentle sands of acceptance after soaring straight over denial, rage, bargaining, and depression.

I realize now that I was in denial even when I typed those sentences. I didn't think he had passed away. I thought he would burst through the door, flinging clothes from his bag while noisily telling me amusing stories about his travels.

I had tried that vault, but it was impossible. Quicksand was what the sands were.

May 27, 2019
Chevy Chase

Tony's backpack was in the hallway at Josh's house, exactly as he had left it. He had managed to purchase two fresh linen shirts. Good ones. These beautiful shirts, which he would never wear, still had their tags attached.

Josh, his sister Erica, her husband David, and the grandmother Ellie, all of them drawn and reduced, were in the kitchen. She felt weak as we hugged. She raised a great man, I told her. What a strange thing to say. I don't recall anything else that was said that evening, so I must have had that thinking even as I was saying it.

We were all in disarray. It was late. After some time, Erica and David, who agreed to stay with her, brought Ellie home to her flat in the vicinity. When Ericka, Josh's wife, left her girls off at the airport on the way back from Maine, she promised to pick up Bizu from his boarding school in the morning. Friends living near his school had offered to pick him up and spend the night with them. However, he declined. He had decided to wait in his dorm by himself.

Josh and I leaned back on the couch. His brother had passed away. The love of my life was gone. Each of us had lost a best friend.

Tony and Josh had a close bond, as close as I think brothers can get. I am three years older than Tony, and Josh is the same age as me. When he was just twenty-six, I cradled the bridegroom and his newborn brother. This was not how it was meant to go.

Who will pass away first? It is the theme that Jack and Babette, the married protagonists of Don DeLillo's book White Noise, ask again. I didn't raise that question because I was older and had survived cancer in my forties. I simply thought it would be me.

I took Tony's wallet from a plastic bag at the hospital. A receipt from Bread and Chocolate, a cafe and bakery about a twelve-minute walk from Josh's residence, was inside. Although the time stamp was hazy, it appeared to be 11:16 a.m. Tony would be declared dead on a hospital gurney in just one hour and twenty-two minutes after he requested that bill.

He had written me that final email at around ten thirty the previous evening. It was the humorous, gossipy one about his Waterford escapades that day. He had already left for the cafe when I read it in the morning. He didn't see my response. He had most likely slept in before going out for a leisurely brunch. According to the receipt, he had coffee, a big OJ, and a Classic Shakshuka. His final supper on this planet. After paying the bill, he exited the café, went back toward his brother's house for two minutes, and then passed out. He must have been holding the crumpled newspaper in the plastic bag when he collapsed. The piece arguing for enslavement reparations was lengthy. Tony and Josh had a conversation that morning, probably just before he left the house. Tony's previous book, Confederates in the Attic, was about a group of Civil War reenactors Josh had met recently. A strange sight in Lewiston, Maine's streets. They had chuckled when he had called Tony.

Josh had intended to stay behind and assist his daughter in cleaning up her dorm before he received my call. Rather, he had paid a driver $100 to transport him to the Portland airport in time for the final flight to Washington, DC. Months later, he told me that he was anxious to get to the house before I did, in case Tony had left it in a way that offended me. He didn't tell me that night.

Josh and I were weepy, tired, and terrified to try to go asleep as we sagged on his couch. At last, in the wee hours of the morning, I walked upstairs and lay in the bed Tony had slept in the previous evening. As he had left it, it was unmade. Imagining the length of his body and the weight of his head, I buried my face in the pillow. I didn't get any sleep. When she was younger, Josh's wife gathered Madame Alexander dolls. They were arranged on the dresser and gazed at me with wide eyes and an insatiable hunger.

I worried about Bizu, who was by himself in his small dorm room. I hoped he wasn't guilty of staying in school. The idea of him clinging to this grandeur until his aunt could arrive the following morning was difficult.

And Nathaniel, who would arrive in Sydney shortly. I had left messages for my sister to call me because I couldn't get through to her there. Before starting work as a biotech entrepreneur in Boston in mid-June, Nathaniel was embarking on a six-month post-college trip with his partner, which would culminate in Australia. In a few more weeks, he would return home in time for Tony's 61st birthday on June 9. It was the longest time father and son had been apart. They would never see each other.

However, I wouldn't be the one to inform Nathaniel of this. After I missed two calls, the first message he received on his phone when he landed in Sydney was a text from a friend from Vineyard:

Really loved your pops.

My sister hadn't seen my messages when she woke up since she was in a hurry to get to an early-morning tennis match. Sobbing, Nathaniel and his girlfriend arrived at the door.

My phone lit up with a message from her just before daybreak. Could she call me? Was I awake? I advised against it, just in case Josh had managed to slip into a precarious sleep in the adjacent bedroom.

She wanted to be by my side and board a plane with Nathaniel. I requested that she wait.

I suspect this gets harder, I wrote. I'll need you more then.

Flinders Island

I discovered I hadn't planned as well as I had assumed and was lacking some necessary ingredients when I began to prepare dinner. I walked back to Whitemark on Friday, just before the business closed at 5:30 p.m., because I wasn't sure if the island's only grocery had weekend hours.

Down on the dock, a weekly cookout was underway. Most of the attendees were island tourists, a rugged-looking, weathered bunch dressed in fleeces and woolens. Since there is fishing, kayaking, and bushwalking to do here, they would come. They were obviously enjoying the meats and salads, which came from the island's farms. Like those in Martha's Vineyard, I would be friends with the young farmers who produced this food if I lived here. I had a sneaking suspicion that it was the same mix: idealistic newcomers dedicated to organic and regenerative practices, and the offspring of multigenerational agricultural families. One advantage of small areas, particularly islands, is that you ultimately get to know everyone. You get to know a much greater variety of people than you would in crowded, class- and income-segregated urban districts.

Even though it's windy, the rain has stopped, and it's clear that the sunset will be spectacular from the Whitemark dock. The horizon is clear, but there are huge cumulonimbus and cirrostratus cloud billows higher up. The conditions are ideal. The pier would be the ideal spot to enjoy it, but I can't remain because of the bad road and the abundance of wildlife after twilight. One of those depressing tangles of fur and bone splattered into the gravel is not something I want to be accountable for. I'll have to watch the show from the road as much as possible.

We were sunset experts, Tony and I. From early summer through the mild fall in the Vineyard, we would get together with friends on Wednesday nights for a picnic and swim at Lambert's Cove beach. In contrast to the harsher ocean beaches to the south, this crescent-shaped area of white sand on the island's north shore faces west and is a good place to swim. Sunset-judging was the night's last activity. Tony would offer the commentary after we gave out points ranging from one to ten: "Just six? The infamously severe Australian judge. The German judge's nine? There, officials suspect graft."

Tony and I discussed how we would be sure to have a west-facing porch with a set of rocking rockers when we grew old. We would dedicate our time to observing sunsets, and we would never miss a spectacular one.

However, we believed we were years away from that. In the middle of our life's journey, we thought we were where we were supposed to be. Certainly much over the Dantean age of thirty-five, but still anticipating a lengthy and fascinating journey to come. There's so much more fun to be had and so much more work to do. Together.

Rather, mi ritrovai por una selva oscura, and I am alone in that forest at dusk.

I'm not sure if the sunset was a ten or not. The western sky is hidden behind the bluff behind the shack, which faces east. It's over when I get back.

At least I don't run across a wombat on the way home.

It rains heavily again the following morning. I decided to light the wood stove because the temperature is significantly below normal for this time of year. The pile is now wet, and I regret not thinking to bring in any wood. Starting the stove is a bother. It is too damp to gather any kindling, and there is none. I lit some ancient coals with candle wax. I take a short stroll on the beach when the rain stops, but it's muddy, so I'm relieved to head back toward the swirl of woodsmoke rising from the shack's chimney. A single pademelon is grazing at the entryway, taking advantage of the rain break. She looks at me with a slender face. I halt abruptly, reprimanded. The trespasser is me. I'm putting things off. I'm putting off what I came here to do by tinkering with the woodstove and preparing food to last me the next few days.

I have to start working.

May 28, 2019
Chevy Chase

I finally dozed off in fits as the sky grew lighter. I had a dream about Tony once. He was there, alive. The dream had no dark edges and was warm and loving.

For one or two minutes, everything felt normal after I woke up. He was still alive. How absurd it was to think that. The dream was yesterday.

Then I woke up completely. It was my second time losing him.

An overwhelming day; a restless night. Friends brought food. Concerning funeral arrangements, some inquired. Both food and funerals were things I didn't want to discuss. I couldn't imagine having to deal with a crowd of people, no matter how adored. When I told Tony's sister Erica that I couldn't picture doing anything just yet, she started crying. She stated that she couldn't simply return home and resume her job as if nothing had occurred. She is the older sister, the mature presence around her younger brothers, a sensitive soul, a loving mother, and an idealistic public defender. My rabbi also concurred with her. "Our community at home longed to express their grief and offer their condolences," she said gently.

But how could I possibly consider catering platters, locations, and lodging? I was unable to. Not quite yet.

The Sydney Morning Herald, The Wall Street Journal, The Washington Post, and The New York Times all had obit writers. My journalist pals handled much of this at these newspapers, but I had some questions to address.

I kept forgetting things. that Tony had just served as the Society of American Historians' president, a position he had enjoyed. Then one of his former employers' newspapers. I had to keep returning calls, sending emails, and fixing my mistakes. A reporter inquired about Tony's Brown graduation date. It wasn't until graduate school that I met him. I was aware that during his junior year of college, he had taken a leave of absence to work for the Frontier Nursing Service in Hyden, Kentucky, where he drove midwives into isolated hollows to provide care to some of the poorest citizens in the nation. His class had graduated, but he had not. But really, when did he?

His cardiologist then called him.

I was desperate to talk to this man. It was so difficult for me to talk to him.

How had he allowed this to occur?

Tony had a cardiologist because he had excessive cholesterol and inherited hypertension. Two months before his death, he had a check-up. He always refused dessert and detested butter, cream, and fatty foods, but he still needed blood pressure medication and statins. We had no reason to think that these problems wouldn't be handled as well for him as they had been for his mother, who was 90 years old. Nine years had passed since he had seen this doctor for the first time. Back then, he had undergone a thorough workup and stress test, and nothing alarming had been found.

I now know his most recent visit wasn't totally ordinary. According to the cardiologist, Tony had visited him with a dyspnea complaint. He once sprinted toward a train. And I recalled the scenario as the cardiologist described it. I remembered Tony jumping out of our stopped Uber at the end of our last trip to Washington, DC, for Passover, and running toward Union Station. He had to meet his editor in New York, but he was late for the train. I was flying home with Bizu, and we were both grinning as we watched him weave and dodge through the automobiles, his wheelie bag raised high above his head. It makes sense that when he collapsed in his seat on the Acela, he was out of breath. Who wouldn't be?

However, he had experienced dyspnea again while playing tennis a few days later. He had casually brought this up to me. He responded that considering he worked six days a week, it felt strange. The cardiologist told me that Tony had been more concerned about this than he had admitted. He was so concerned he sought his doctor's advice.

It was a routine examination. His lungs were clear, his EKG was normal, and I saw no signs of jugular inflammation.

In addition to recommending a complete workup and a series of more conclusive tests, the doctor claimed to have adjusted Tony's medication. However, they discovered that there was not a single day that could accommodate all of the required tests when they examined the calendar of days remaining before his book tour. The two full days it would take to trek back and forth to Boston were time that Tony didn't want to waste. There were a ton of minor things that looked urgent, like pre-publicity work and scheduling decisions for his time on the road. After the trip was done, they had scheduled all the required appointments and decided on a date.

Inscribed on Tony's calendar, there it was: MED TESTS on June 21.

It is 25 days too late. For what reason had they waited? Why the deadly delay?

I was unsure of how to respond to this physician. I was worried what I might say. After he got the autopsy results, we decided to talk again. Weeks later, shortly after that March checkup, I stumbled over this tweet while nostalgically going through Tony's:

Cardiologists are a hard-hearted lot. As one just told me: "I can give you a battery of tests, tell you all's fine, and the warranty on that is the time it takes you to get to the parking lot, where you could drop dead from a heart attack."

Was it why those tests had seemed less urgent to him?

Bizu and his aunt came that afternoon. He had a default attitude in his mid-teens that was best described as a protective crouch, ready to swat away our controlling parental wing. A stoic child who, in a family full of oversharers and blabbermouths, usually talked far less than he thought.

My son sobbed as he collapsed into my arms. After leaving the house, we strolled hand in hand to the location where Tony had fallen. Josh's neighborhood is a long-established area with cozy homes, gardens abounding with springtime bloom, and old trees. We made our way to Northampton Street amid dappled shadows. It wasn't very far. As we stood there, we gazed at the ordinary squares of white concrete. It was difficult to understand how something so devastating and significant could have occurred in such a commonplace location.

I muttered, "He loved you so much." "He was really pleased with you." That year, Bizu had prospered. He had picked difficult classes and excelled in them. During our recent visit to his school, teachers who wanted to commend he approached Tony and me.

Jennifer Senior cites a therapist in her essay "On Grief" who compares those who have experienced loss to travelers on an aircraft that has collided with a hilltop and needs to descend. No one can help the others; everyone has shattered bones. Each must defeat it on their own. My sons have their own tales to share. I'm not going to do that here. All I can say is that I had no idea how alone Bizu's journey would be or how little I could do to aid him when he was sagging against me on the street corner.

The DC medical examiner left a message for us when we returned home. I had to go downtown and identify Tony's body for them. I was perplexed by this because I had been told that I couldn't see him until the autopsy was completed and the body was given to a funeral home.

"But if I can't see his body, how will I get an ID?"

"You'll do it using a picture."

This is not the intended course of events. I had prepared myself for the zip of a body bag, metal cabinets, and delicate morgue staff. I was prepared for that. Since that would be him, at least. At least I would be able to touch him and be by his side at last.

But I was denied even that little consolation.

I scheduled a time to complete the ID. To find out the results of the autopsy, friends who have friends in the DC bureaucracy set up a meeting with the medical examiner. We would have had to wait weeks to receive the report, so this was a huge favor.

Together, Josh and I slid down. Like every other DC office, it was a shiny glass and steel skyscraper. There is no visible indication of the

suffering that exists within. After going through security, we were seated in a room that looked like a high-end doctor's office and had blond furnishings. A young woman with gel fingernails adorned with stars and Fulani braids gave me a clipboard with a passport-sized photo, face down,.
"You can turn it over and make the identification when you're ready," she replied.
I'd never be prepared.
He had a horrible appearance. He appeared to have had a difficult time. which he had, of course. He was still Tony, though. I touched his face with my hand.
I apologize. I apologize for not taking better care of you. Apologies for not being with you. I'm sorry, but I can't join you right now.
That Monday, I could have been with him. I could have taken him to see his old friends in Waterford, walked with him to breakfast, held him in my arms as he passed away, or flown down to Washington for the long weekend.
I had decided not to go for several reasons. A close buddy on the island was having a huge birthday celebration, and we had spent the previous week together in Nashville. Tony had been making fun of me for putting off finishing my manuscript, saying things like, "Horse not exactly galloping to the finish line."
Additionally, the few flights that were available on Memorial Day were inconvenient, making travel to and from the island a major hassle. I had decided to stay. I will always regret that choice.
I filled out the forms and created the ID that the starry fingers had put in front of me. We then awaited the arrival of the medical examiner.
He was a trim, kind man who was skilled at discussing difficult subjects. Josh was especially skilled at listening, having served as the liaison for numerous family medical emergencies. He had been there for Tony and me when Nathaniel's birth had descended into an obstetrical crisis. With an Apgar score of one at birth, Nathaniel was taken by a crash team to the neonatal intensive care unit, where our small baby was hooked up to IVs and oxygen. Tony's father had

accused us of selecting a midwife to perform the delivery rather than the ob-gyn he had suggested. Josh was the one who soothed him and helped us all get through it.

According to the medical examiner, he initially believed that Tony's death was caused by obstruction of the left anterior descending coronary artery. The LAD, the body's largest artery, provides half the blood flow to the heart muscle. In cases of abrupt death like Tony's, this artery is typically suspected, much like a criminal with a lengthy criminal history. We call it the widow-maker. However, only 60% of LAD was blocked, the autopsy found. Normally, a stent wouldn't even be indicated by that level of occlusion. According to the examiner, he now believes Tony's vascular condition might have been unintentional. To look into another suspicion, he requested microscopic sections, which would require some time to prepare and assess.

Thus, we were still in the dark. However, I appreciated his concern and his perseverance in finding a solution.

Flinders Island

unexpected guests. When I look up, I see an old woman walking slowly across my terrace while leaning on a cane. It's shocking. The few individuals I have spotted out here have been distant dots far down the beach. What's even more startling is that she knocks and throws an empty shopping bag at me as I open the door.
"I apologize for keeping it for so long."
"But I don't own it."
"Well, this is where it belongs." Then she leaves.
I still can't figure out where she may have come from when Mick shows up, greeted by a shiny young kelpie and an elderly-looking cattle dog. He claims to be the shack's owner, a farmer, and he has just stopped over to make sure I don't run out of gas and water.
He has been on the island for twenty years and has a deep farmer tan and windswept blond hair. I want to ask him a million things, but because he seems like a busy man, I limit it to this: How is the island defending itself against overdevelopment?
He claims that "people here are pretty unified about preserving it." In terms of tourism, he argues, they're at a bit of a sweet spot: Since the airfare from Melbourne costs $620, swarms of backpackers are excluded, and there are no five-star hotels here for the yuppies. He ignores the absurdly beautiful view of the sea and mountains behind him and gestures toward the hut, saying, "They aren't going to want a place like this." "Isn't there a restroom out back?" He gives a sly smile. The restroom is located at the rear, with a view of the water and a shabby snorkel that doubles as a toilet roll holder.
After letting Mick finish his work, I happen to look down at my attire. I've been wearing the same old T-shirt and shabby shorts every day. I comb my hair with my hand. Unrinsed salt from swimming in the ocean starches it. I'd never be confused for a yuppie, for sure. Since the mirror is in the outdoor shower and I haven't used it yet, I hadn't noticed how I looked. Five days have passed.

The mourner does not shave or cut his hair, nor does he bathe or shower for pleasure, during shivah. Laundering or wearing freshly laundered clothes is also prescribed.... It is a time-honored tradition to cover the mirrors.

Although I haven't meant to, it appears that I have adhered to these rules.

I became a Jew just before we were married because I didn't want to be the last in a long line that had survived the Shoah and pogroms. Tony was a Jew. We honored Passover, the High Holidays, Sukkot, Hanukkah, and occasionally a special dinner with candles on Friday evenings. Our children attended Hebrew school. However, we were not religious, and our ties to the customs were based on family and culture. I would have had a roadmap through my mourning, dictating exactly what I needed to do and when, if we had been observant Jews. In Orthodox Judaism, grieving is divided into stages. The period between death and burial is the most intense, aninut. Grief is described as "stupefyingly intense" during aninut. Since the mourner is in no condition to be comforted, she should not even be given condolences. It is expected of bystanders to discreetly assist with the practical aspect of funeral ceremonies. I was rushing to board aircraft and vessels during my aninut. I called my husband's publicist and argued with the medical staff about seeing his body. Any chance of letting my sadness be "stupefyingly intense" had been overshadowed by my instinct to do these actions and my belief in their importance.

A Jewish mourner sits after burial. She spends seven days at home, doing little more than taking sympathy calls and thinking back on the life of the deceased. Every day, the bereaved come together with a minyan (ten men for Orthodox) to sing kaddish, the death prayer that makes no mention of death. It is a period of total detachment from the outside world and its expectations. One "gets up" from shiva and resumes their regular activities on the morning of the seventh day. The mourner typically goes on their first walk outside the house with friends. However, the mourner refrains from wearing or purchasing new clothing, getting their haircut, listening to music, and participating in any festivities for an additional thirty days, known as sheloshim. The thirty-day period is regarded as the end of a spouse's mourning observance. While parents may have several spouses, children, or siblings, the tie with a parent is unique, hence children are the only bereaved who must do a complete year of mourning rites. I'm saddened to hear that only biological parents need to be grieved, not adoptive ones. It appears to be an unjust devaluation of parent, child, and the boundless potential for love.

It is required of Jews to strictly adhere to these rules, but not to go beyond them. The goal is to give people a way to express their grief while simultaneously offering a structure for coping with the loss and continuing with life.

In contrast to Jews, who restrict mourners to a select group of close relatives (spouses, parents, siblings), First Nations people in Australia have a completely different stance. It is believed that grief affects the entire community of the deceased in this 50,000-year-old culture with the world's oldest religion. Everyone in traditional societies is ostensibly related by given kinships that specify privileges, obligations, and even who is allowed to marry whom.

Therefore, when someone passes away, everyone in that community participates in what is known as "Sorry Business," even if it requires traveling a considerable distance. Another cycle of deep sadness is triggered by each new arrival. Weeks may pass between ceremonies. According to Northern Territory elder Miriam-Rose Ungunmerr-Baumann, "we wait a long time with sorrow when a relation dies." "We take responsibility for our sorrow and let it gradually heal." (Creative Spirits, "Mourning an Aboriginal Death: Sorry Business.")

In Islam, a widow practices iddah, which is a partial separation from the outside world for three or four months. She can go to work and take care of her needs, but she shouldn't go out, get dressed, or interact with people in any other way. She is not allowed to make any marriage-related agreements at this time. I've read testimonies from contemporary Muslim widows who support and oppose iddah. One person commented about how it provided her with the justification she needed to keep quiet and to herself since she was being pressured to be social by well-meaning people before she was ready. Another reported feeling ridiculed whenever she even made a joke or smiled in public. In private, she cried and mourned for her husband, she admitted to an interviewer. She didn't need instructions on when or how to grieve him.

The majority of religious traditions erect barriers around the bereaved, providing guidelines for what to do during times of extreme confusion when everything seems to have fallen apart. For the third, seventh, and forty days following burial, there are particular observances in Islam. I went to a shab-e haft, or seventh-night service, for a 90-year-old matriarch while working as a reporter in Tehran. I sat in the women's courtyard wearing my black chador. A mullah with a melodic voice sang a lengthy and melancholic song praising mothers after reciting passages from the Koran from the neighbor's home, where the men had assembled. A loudspeaker mounted on the wall separating the courtyard piped this to our group.

The women shed tears. Not all tears were shed for the dead. There was much for these women to be sad about. A young woman who had just been released from seven years as a political prisoner for shouting "Death to Khomeini!" was in this courtyard, along with mothers who had lost boys in the protracted war with Iraq and a mother who had witnessed a son being murdered for joining an anti-revolutionary terrorist cell. Regardless of one's political views, there was a space for unfettered expression of grief.

I had written about Ayatollah Khomeini's funeral a year ago. The city's roads had turned into rivers of black, as I could see from the Huey helicopter that took reporters to the grave site. Black-clad mourners were marching southward to the burial place down every major road and alleyway, chanting prayers, wailing, and beating their breasts and brows until they occasionally bled. As the entire nation marked chehelom, or the fortieth day following his funeral, forty days later, I received an invitation to return to Tehran. On that occasion, one grieves once more with the same fervor as on the first day. However, things go back to normal the next day. People would no longer be expected to dress in black, and all black flags would be taken down from Tehran's public areas. Islamic mourning had a known end, regardless of the deceased's prominence or the depth of the loss.

I spent years carrying my pass for the Khomeini family women's section in my wallet, and the service I went to was conducted in a sports arena. I reasoned that it might be my escape card from the cellar if I were ever kidnapped by some radical organizations.

The ninth day following death is important to Filipino Catholics since it is when mourners reassemble to pray. Hindus grieve deeply for thirteen days following a cremation. In addition to avoiding holy places and abiding by other taboos that distinguish the mourning time from daily life, mourners are viewed as impure. For seven weeks, Buddhists do prayers and rituals for the deceased every seven days. The deceased's spirit is believed to transition to its next incarnation following the ceremony on the 49th day.

As long as it takes to collect the materials for the complex cremation procedure required to transfer the spirit from this life to the next, bodies are interred in Bali's Hindu and animist traditions. Wives have a lot of demanding ceremonial tasks to complete, but they accomplish them in the company of their loved ones and the community, which serves as a continual reminder that even if one aspect of their lives has been taken away, many other bonds of attachment still exist. The tone is joyful and celebratory of the soul's liberation by the time the colorful procession to the cremation site occurs, which may happen weeks or months later.

Janet De Neefe describes how Balinese traditions lessen the sting of death's finality in her memoir Fragrant Rice. She describes how her husband's late mother was thought to have reincarnated as her first child, Dewi. The woman's elderly friends showed up as soon as a priest made that announcement, holding the infant, referring to her by her previous name, telling her how much they had missed her, and updating her on their lives since her passing.

Besides not believing in reincarnation, Tony also did not believe in a hereafter. Death, he thought, was the end. I also think so. However, since his death, things have happened that I am unable to understand. I was contacted by one of his cousins shortly after his passing. At one of Tony's final book readings, this young woman, who had been cut off from the majority of the family for years, reestablished a cordial relationship with him close to her West Coast residence. She sent an email stating that she had established a memorial garden for Tony at her house with flowers in the hues of yellow and red after consulting her psychic, who had a vision of Tony standing on the edge of a cliff surrounded by masses of those flowers. I said, "How nice," and didn't give it any more thought.

I realized that I had gone through all four seasons without him when a swarm of tulips showed up in my own garden the following spring, precisely one year after his passing. Others have glossy red and yellow variegated petals, lipstick red, and chrome yellow. I never grow tulips because the bulbs are too frequently eaten by squirrels. Additionally, I had solely used white and delicate lilac bushes to build that border. And yet there they are, spring after spring, tulips as vividly yellow and blazing red as traffic lights. Unfathomable.

Tony would sneer, I know. And he would probably disagree with my desire to create my own mourning custom here on Flinders. He would at least find a way to make fun of it.

I picture myself like he would, unkempt and alone myself, washed up on a beach at the end of the world, commemorating memorial days that have no set length. He's smiling, amused, I can see. "You crazy woman, what do you think you're doing? Go to the pub, for heaven's sake!

I shake my head, but I return his smile. Finally, I'm giving myself permission to wait a long time with my grief.

to endure it for however long it takes.

May 28, 2019
Chevy Chase

The first day without him seemed to go on forever. Ultimately, it ended on a bizarre note.

The day following the publication of his book, Tony had recorded an interview for PBS NewsHour. Like many authors, he had hoped it would air during the brief period when publishers pay booksellers to keep copies prominent in bookstores—the New Release table's prime real estate. After taping, Tony had been nervous the next few days. He was well aware that soft features, such as book interviews, that had a clear news hook may go weeks without airing due to the strain of breaking news.

His passing made headlines. We all gathered in front of Josh and Erica's big TV in their den. Tony's author photo, which was taken in our paddock with one of our large-eyed alpacas looking over his shoulder, filled the screen. Like an inscription on a gravestone, across the bottom of the screen:

Tony Horwitz
1958–2019

Judy Woodruff stated, "Tonight, we finally remember and hear from author and Pulitzer Prize–winning journalist Tony Horwitz." Yesterday he died unexpectedly after what appeared to be a heart arrest. Confederates in the Attic, which examines contemporary Southern perspectives on the Civil War and those who recreate it, is Horwitz's most well-known work. It was a best-selling novel. He worked as a correspondent for The Wall Street Journal, covering wars in the Balkans, the Middle East, and Africa. For his 1995 Pulitzer Prize-winning series on economic disparity and low-wage occupations, such as laboring in Southern chicken processing facilities, he received. Horwitz uses first-person accounts to tell the story in several of his books. That's the case with Spying on the South, his latest book. He recently had a conversation with William Brangham. That interview is here. It was nearly amazing to see him: charming and lively. I was so engrossed in watching him that I briefly forgot the situation. He was skilled at delivering the best anecdotes from the book while speaking in short bursts. He described how, while attempting to purge the overloaded bookcases in our barn, he had reconnected with an old undergraduate work, Frederick Law Olmsted's The Cotton Kingdom. Many years before he discovered his calling as the creator of Central Park and other famous landscapes, Olmsted worked as a reporter for The New York Times. In the years leading up to the Civil War, he was dispatched to the South to examine the widening rifts in the country. Tony described how he had chosen to retrace Olmsted's excursions, contrasting what Fred had observed at the time with what he discovered now, after being struck by the parallels with this current period of American split.

Given how similar Fred and Tony were in their reporting style—don't go to big shots and experts—it was a brilliant notion. Ask ordinary people about their lives and report from scratch. Examine significant topics while also finding humor in commonplace situations. It was an excellent novel.

But at what price? Reporting it, Tony pushed himself to the limit. It was nothing new for him to push to the edge. However, as he grew older, he found it more difficult to maintain the frenzied energy required to persuade strangers to allow him to labor alongside them on a coal barge on the Ohio River, to mingle with monster-truck enthusiasts at a debauch known as Mudfest in Louisiana, or to ride a mule across Hill Country Texas. Tony ended up in the emergency room for a month after suffering a concussion from his mule. Naturally, he embraced the moniker "Rhinestone Jewboy" and transformed even that terrible incident into a humorous, self-deprecating chapter.

Then came the writing, which was always a demanding task for Tony but was accelerated this time by a tight deadline and a demanding publishing schedule. He drank gallons of coffee, chewed packs of Nicorette gum, and nibbled on Provigil, a medication designed to keep fighter pilots alert, to finish the book on time. As a result, he would write till the middle of the day, then spend an hour at the gym, smash the StairMaster, and use a pump iron. Return home, continue chewing Nicorette, and wait another hour or two.

He used alcohol at night to counter all stimulants. He fell asleep as a result, but was awakened early in the morning. He would then get up, have more wine, and respond to all the emails he hadn't had time to do during the day.

A lot of wine.

I was probably going to be the one in our family with a drinking problem if anyone did. Drunks swung from every branch of my family tree. My dad had an alcohol problem. His parents were, too. Although my mother didn't drink, her mother did, and on numerous occasions, we would return home to find my mother's uncle Oscar unconscious on the front veranda, smelling as strong as a brewery. To get over my crippling shyness, I began drinking while I was in college. Later, when Sydney newsrooms were drowning in alcohol, I went to work as a reporter. However, I became less dependent on alcohol as my confidence grew, and my decline into dissipation was further halted by my relocation to the United States and the more austere newsroom atmosphere of The Wall Street Journal. That, and my family's example. They weren't all fun drunks. Drinking could make my beautiful grandmother and my wonderful dad mean, even hideous.

Tony was unique. He had engaged in the degeneracies of the day as an undergraduate in the early 1980s—too much alcohol and too many psychedelics—until a bad trip turned him off. He had cut back on his excess by the time I met him, and he was just a boisterous social drinker. I could count on one hand the number of times in the past 35 years that I witnessed him inebriated and clumsy.

As foreigners, we could purchase alcohol while we lived in Cairo, but it was not worth the hassle and required a ton of paperwork. We would play countless games of Basra, a fast-paced card game Tony discovered in an Iraqi coffee shop, in the dining room of our hot apartment—the air conditioning never completely worked—during our little leisure between missions. Sometimes we'd split a bottle of dirty Egyptian beer. It wasn't an issue when we had to report in arid nations like Saudi Arabia, Libya, and Iran and had to do without anything at all.

In Sydney and London, where the drinking culture is more likely to encourage intemperance, we were less abstinent. However, it was something you did with pals around a table on the weekends. It wasn't a daily routine or an intense necessity, but rather a pleasurable release. That changed while he was writing and reporting his latest book. Because of his drinking, he lost the off switch. Until the bottle was emptied, he would continue. I began keeping an eye on him at social gatherings to make sure we departed before he went too far.

He was aware that this could not continue. He said he would definitely stop it. following the book tour. No more nicotine, alcohol, or medications. He would reset his system and cleanse. When he recognized he might need help, he asked his cardiologist and others who had joined the wagon for suggestions on how to taper off his drinking. We discussed ideas for a future undertaking that wouldn't necessitate the same level of extreme mental and physical craziness.

I eagerly anticipated the day this new chapter would be turned over. I started looking at spas. We would depart together following his book tour. We would eat raw vegetables for three weeks or even a month without alcohol. We would swim and go up mountains. Do yoga, perhaps. We would return home with new routines. Across the field from our house was our next-door neighbor's spacious studio, where she taught yoga. Perhaps we would become one of those gorgeous elderly couples with calm grins and yoga mats beneath their arms.All of this would occur. All we needed to do was finish the book tour.

Flinders Island

I get up early to witness the sunrise, which first silvers the concave curves of the clouds before turning them roseate and scattering pink petals across the sky.

I've made the decision to return to Wybalenna and leave the shack today. When Tony and I arrived here in 2000, I was researching the novel I planned to write at the time, and this was one of the locations we visited on the island.

I no longer wanted to travel off on lengthy, open-ended newspaper trips to risky locations after the birth of our son Nathaniel in 1996. Tony was the one who persuaded me to write fiction. I was fundamentally a reporter. I had spent the most of my life wanting to do it. I had become proficient at it. I was completely unsure about my ability to make stuff up. However, Tony urged me to give it a shot, and so I penned Year of Wonders, my debut book. That book was on the verge of publication when we traveled to Flinders, and my editor had urged me to suggest another.

I made the decision to base my second book on the life of Jane Franklin, a daughter of an English silk merchant who arrived in Tasmania in 1837 as the governor's wife. After being sent to Sydney, Tasmania was the penal colony of last resort for prisoners who committed new crimes. It was known for the terrible atrocities committed against Indigenous people, who were hunted down and killed, and the few survivors were sent to Flinders Island. It was a location where cruelty was compounded and radiated. In the end, Jane Franklin's persistent efforts to stop these injustices resulted in her husband's recall.

As a young reporter investigating environmental issues for The Sydney Morning Herald, I had met Jane. I rafted down the Franklin River, which bears her husband's name, with politicians and environmentalists. The river is wild and picturesque from source to mouth and was in danger of being dammed at the time for a negligible amount of hydroelectric power.

The river ran through a true wilderness, which is an old-growth rainforest that is impenetrable by humans and covered in horizontal scrub. For a city dweller who was unfamiliar with camping, the trip was taxing. I learnt how to lug my equipment over steep, slick riverbanks and paddle for my life over thunderous rapids while we were each in our own little inflatable raft. I slept in a sagging tent in pouring rain, ached in muscles I didn't even know I had, and smelled like a wet sheep in my army surplus woolens.

It was a journey that changed my life. I have never been in a place where nature is vast and humans are tiny. I realized that my human body and brain had evolved to survive in the wilderness for thousands of years, and that the only life I had ever known—in a busy city—was a highly abnormal environment for my species.

One of the conservationists came out of the bush one evening when we were camping beneath the magnificent Rock Island Bend, carrying a clutch of leaves. He turned over the shiny blade of a laurel, the delicate fronds of a Huon pine, and the serrated leaves of a celery top, saying, "I thought you might like to know what the trees are." For days, I had been staring at the same trees with little distinction. Suddenly, I had a fresh perspective on my surroundings.

The untamed areas of Tasmania and the young campaigners battling to preserve them captured my heart. I began to consider relocating there, sacrificing my journalistic neutrality to work as a wilderness activist and support the fledgling Green Party of the nation. Then I found out that I had been awarded the Greg Shackleton scholarship at Columbia University, which is named for a courageous young journalist who was killed by the Indonesian army during the East Timor invasion.

The fight to build the Franklin dam was coming to a head. As thousands gathered to roadblock the dam site, I was hesitant to leave the narrative behind. However, I was enticed by Columbia, a master's degree, and an adventure in New York. It was my "sliding-door" moment: Tasmanian conservationist or international correspondent? My life changed completely after accepting the scholarship, meeting Tony, and landing a job at The Wall Street Journal.

However, the untamed scenery of Tasmania and Jane Franklin's tale remained in my memory. As the most traveled lady of her generation, Jane had lived a full life within the confines of the Georgian era. When she traveled with prisoner porters through the Franklin River valley, she caused a stir in the colony. Her spirit of adventure and her advocacy for Aboriginal people and women convicts drew me in.

Therefore, Tony and I had left our bed and breakfast on a windy morning to travel to Wybalenna, which is a key location in her story. Regardless of whose byline ended up on the final piece, we frequently reported together throughout our years as foreign journalists stationed in Cairo and London. As symbiotic in our professional lives as the fungus and algae that combine to form the vibrant orange Caloplaca, we were each other's second set of eyes and ears. Editors started calling us Hobro in news meetings by the conclusion of our time at The Wall Street Journal, and that's how we increasingly viewed ourselves. Basically one individual, beyond partners.

As book writers, we kept up this symbiotic relationship by exchanging ideas, reading each other's drafts, and exchanging expertise. Tony's skill at searching through archives and his brutal editing were helpful to me. He would use a pen slash to eliminate my favorite words. He was particularly upset with me for using the terms "desiccated" and "gnarled" excessively. He kept throwing them out, and they started infiltrating my prose.

I could help him depict the natural world more precisely than he does with his favorite descriptors, "bush," "flower," and "tree." Occasionally, I offered a helpful narrative twist or a line of investigation that he hadn't considered. We joined each other on research trips whenever possible, serving as a second set of eyes and ears to pick up details. He accompanied me to Wybalenna for that reason.

Aboriginal people have defended their lands by fighting to the death in numerous locations, using spears against firearms. I doubt that any other location is as eerily haunted as Wybalenna.

This was a slow-motion massacre in which victims perished while living in exile. One strategy used by Aborigines to avoid capture on the mainland of Tasmania was to abduct their children and promise to return them only after the parents traveled to Flinders Island. One chief gave up after years of fighting after his daughter was taken. She died in a Hobart orphanage and was never returned to him. Before passing away from illness and despair in Wybalenna, he and his wife had another daughter, Mathinna.

The settlement's name translates to "Black People's Houses," and when Jane Franklin visited Wybalenna, she noticed a row of twenty homes that were out of place on this windswept stretch of coastal heathland, packed together like a London slum. She sent for Mathinna, the six-year-old girl she had met there, after her second visit. Mathinna was taken from her remaining family and brought to Government House in Hobart, where she was nurtured alongside Eleanor, the seventeen-year-old daughter of the Franklins. For a while, the youngster seemed to have been a complete member of the family, dressed in a scarlet gown with puff sleeves, driven around in the viceregal carriage, and asked to sit for a portrait. Mathinna wrote in a heartfelt letter: "I have pen and ink because I am a decent little girl. Yes, I adore my dad. I have a petticoat, a shift, and a doll. I'm wearing a red dress. I'm glad even if my feet, shoes, and stockings hurt.

Jane Franklin left Mathinna at the same Hobart orphanage where her older sister had died in 1843 after John Franklin was called back to England. Jane took this action despite being aware of the place's overcrowding, disease, hunger, and severe penalties. She didn't even abandon her doll for the girl. (A descendant of Eleanor's recently bequeathed it to an English museum.) When Mathinna was unable to adapt, she was sent back to Flinders Island, and when that desolate community was completely abandoned, she and the few remaining people moved to another desolate location close to Hobart. There, at age 20, she drowned. Jane Franklin is not known to have ever asked about her.

Understanding how your characters justify their own behavior to themselves is one of the most important skills a novelist can have. There was no way for me to think of the excuse Jane Franklin had given herself for leaving that child behind. I finally came to the conclusion that I couldn't write a novel on her as I couldn't access her thoughts.

I was just starting to get the gist of the narrative on my first trip to Wybalenna with Tony. I saw drifts of miniature iris blossoming between the superintendent's house and the settlement chapel as we strolled through the windswept area of gently sloping grasses. It was not a natural flower, but an English one. I picked up a corm, wrapped it in moist tissue, and took it home to Sydney to plant in my garden.

In my mind, I saw a superintendent's wife from the nineteenth century digging up corms of her favorite iris in her English garden and transporting them to Tasmania. Maybe she was excited about the trip, anticipating the garden she would create. Maybe she was scared. I don't think she could have predicted the suffering she would see.

The following spring, when the iris flowered in my yard in Sydney, I brought up our trip to Flinders Island with Tony. "The land is still inexpensive, and it's really lovely there. One day, I hope to have enough money to purchase a block. With a noncommittal grunt, he swiftly shifted the topic.

When I come here, the irises are not in flower. The summer is too late. The fields are stretches of sun-bleached grass with delicate golden tints. I make my way to the cemetery where a large number of unmarked Aboriginal people rest. However, a marker honors Elizabeth Milligan, the superintendent's wife, who died at the age of nineteen, "one day after her confinement."

I've come to the correct spot if the goal is to grieve.

May 29, 2019
Chevy Chase

Tony's body was eventually turned over to the funeral director by the medical examiner. Josh had kept the modest, unpretentious funeral home his pragmatic father had chosen before his own passing in 2012. It was also the choice Josh's wife made for her father, who died five years later at age 86.

Tony's father passed away from Parkinson's disease complications at the age of 87. At ninety, Tony's mother was still going strong. How much trust has been misplaced in these parents' lifespan! We thought that long-lived parents produced long-lived children. Until he was seventy, Dr. Norman Horwitz pulled bullets from spines and removed brain tumors. Up to the final months of his life, he continued to consult on challenging cases at Walter Reed National Military Medical Center despite having a dissected aorta. Norman would be devastated to learn that his youngest child would live 27 years fewer than he did.

There are no elaborate chapels at the funeral parlor. Strictly speaking, they don't even have a viewing room. Those who choose for their streamlined offerings typically don't desire that. However, once Josh gave him the rundown on our predicament, they said we may drop by in the late afternoon.

The crowds had clearly upset Bizu, who spent the majority of the day by my side, the loud conversations, and the stories being told about Tony. He winced at the laughing when the stories were humorous, as was frequently the case. This was obviously not what he was prepared for. I had to take him home. Once more, Nathaniel was in the air, traveling from Sydney to Dallas for fifteen hours, Boston for four more, and finally, the Vineyard for the forty-five-minute puddle jumper. In order for us to get home before he did, I made reservations for an evening flight. On the way to the airport, we would stop at the funeral home.

In an unremarkable strip mall, it was an unremarkable storefront. I gave Bizu a hug and let him wait in the car after asking him if he was certain he didn't want to come inside. A young woman behind the desk in a little workplace. Josh had previously met her when handling his father's and father-in-law's cremations. She led us into a little room hidden behind the office and apologized for the claustrophobic situation. She was kind and genuine.

And there he was. His head was well cushioned, and he was wrapped in a beautiful white blanket with only his face visible. I discovered later, after reading the autopsy report, that this was done to conceal the medical abuse he had endured. However, I was happy to see his face at last.

I gave him a cheek rub. It felt cool, like though he had just emerged from a swim at dusk. His body had been washed, and his hair was still somewhat damp. Unlike the morgue, he no longer appeared battered and gaunt. He was a handsome, happy man in his prime middle years, and he looked just like himself. And he was going to stay that way now.

"My love," I said again and again. "My dear." The woman stopped me when I grabbed for the edge of the white blanket, even though I needed to hold his hand. She said, "Let me just prepare him for that." Josh and I went outside for a while. To be honest, I would have liked to see everything—the autopsy incisions, everything—but I was too weak to oppose her good intentions.

His hands have always captivated me. Large, meaty hands of a peasant. His touch was persistent and full of longing. Before we fell asleep, his arm's weight threw itself over me.

I took his hand. I wanted to hold it forever.

Flinders Island

sulking. That's what it is?
My mother greatly resented wallowing. Move on from yourself. For once, consider other people. Although many aspects of her life would have permitted it, she didn't indulge in self-pity. You went ahead and did it in Gloria's world. Her activity was unrelenting, and her empathy was wide. You made every effort to alter what you could. You didn't waste time moping about things you couldn't do.

I was strongly advised as a child to hold back my tears. Weeping over movies or literature was not acceptable. The Three Lives of Thomasina, a Disney film in which a heartbreaking number of adorable animals suffer terrible endings, was shown at the drive-in when I was around seven years old thanks to my neighbors. I lied and claimed that the neighbors' smoking in the car was the reason my eyes were watery when I arrived home, snotty and red-eyed. The ability to cry whenever I wanted was one of my favorite adult liberties, whether it was during heartfelt films, books, poems, or, heaven forbid, Telstra advertisements. I cried when I saw the weather report, my sister laughed.

Years into my work as a foreign reporter, I was once on the West Bank, driving through Hebron as the school day was coming to an end. To distinguish myself from an Israeli settler, I had the Arabic term for "journalist" printed on my windshield and a Palestinian keffiyeh on my dashboard because I was driving an Israeli rental car with non-Palestinian license plates. However, I swore at myself for making the rookie mistake of driving by a school at that hour when the shebab, the young boys, mobbed my car and began throwing stones and concrete chunks. Metal shattered and windshield broken. One of those rock fragments might crush one more second and my skull. I jumped out and screamed at the children, knowing that was my only option. "Kida, leish? "Anna sahafiyya!" Why on earth? I work as a reporter!

Adults shouted loudly at the lads from surrounding houses, and they immediately scattered, appearing ashamed.

I was led inside and given tea by the adults. I guess shock took over, and I started crying. I shook from head to toe and let out big, heaving sobs that came from deep inside my gut. We don't really mean "hysterical," but this was the real thing. Vexed at my lack of control and ashamed in front of those who lived under military occupation and with some of the most radical Israeli settlers, I sought to pause and gather myself. I had no doubt that my hosts had experienced far more horror than I had. However, my body made a demand for its release that day.

It's the most tears I've shed for Tony. I should have done it as soon as I learned of his passing. However, I was scared to give in to it. I knew that once I started, I might not be able to stop, recalling that day in Hebron and my total lack of self-control. So I turned it off. And I haven't been able to cry for two years.

I followed my mother's advice and considered other people as I drove out of Wybalenna yesterday. In particular, the terrible fate of the children, the deported men, the women who were abducted, and the children who were snatched and then left behind. The heartbroken individuals gazing across the slender strait that divides them from the nourishing lands they cherished. They had been left with nothing; I still had a lot.

Humans pass away. I thought, "I have this in common with every single one of all the thousands of people down there, living their varied, vivid lives," as I gazed out my airplane window at the crowded residences of the Queens borough on the descent to JFK Airport the day following Tony's passing. Even while we may not have much else in common, we do have this. All of us will perish. We'll all be sad. Women lose husbands. Widows everywhere, widows. One of my close friends unexpectedly lost a husband to stroke, while two others lost their husbands to cancer. A text message announcing another shocking death showed up on my phone almost exactly two years to the day I received the devastating news about Tony. An automobile

accident had claimed the life of my goddaughter, a nineteen-year-old who was fiery and radiant. Her life being stolen seemed like a blow from which neither a parent nor a sibling could ever fully recover.
And yet, I was wallowing here.
I switched on the car radio without paying attention. For the entire week, I had heard no news. Shutting out the typical noises was a deliberate aspect of my escape from the outside world. News is my go-to background noise. The BBC and National Public Radio provide the background music for my household. James Coomarasamy and Mary Louise Kelly could also be my roommates. I can listen to the news while cooking, getting coffee, and running errands because the radio is usually on in the kitchen and the car.
"As rescuers search through debris in a race against the cold, the death toll from the massive earthquake in Syria and Turkey, which has already reached 1,500, is expected to rise."
The dead toll quickly increased to 2,600. After a few hours, it had risen to almost 3500.
Throughout the day, they perish. As the snow falls, they perish caught in the debris. They freeze outside bedless hospitals while they wait to be triaged. The reporter is informed by the hospital's sole physician that this is not typical triage. "I am unable to decide which ones I might save. Only those that don't require much resources can be selected for possible saving. We just do not possess them.
They are dying while I swim for a long time on this lovely, deserted beach. They're withering while I sit in the sun drying off. Five thousand people had died by the time I went to bed. The final figure will probably be twenty thousand, a Red Crescent official blurts. Thirty-three thousand soon. Nearly 60,000 souls will be involved in the end.
I am familiar with that part of Turkey. Tony and I both reported from Diyarbakır, a Kurdish city very close to the epicenter. Situated between the anvil of a violent separatist movement and the hammer of the Turkish military, it was a tense site. Following the first Gulf War, it later served as a starting point for journeys into Kurdish Iraq. As a

reporter covering disasters, I had always looked for the one person among many, the one whose narrative, whose personal suffering, a reader could identify with.

A reporter does this while I'm listening to the radio. He tells the story of a distressed father sitting in debris and holding his dead daughter's hand, who is fifteen years old. He can only touch that portion of her. The remainder is crushed beneath slabs of collapsing concrete.

A young guy is interviewed by another reporter as he sifts through ice-rimmed debris in an attempt to reach the kitchen's wreckage, where he knows his mother is imprisoned. He must hope she is still alive, but he worries she is dead. "You know, everyone wants to die a normal death."

With so many deaths, how can I grieve my one loss? I have reason to believe that my one man did not suffer when he passed away.

He died. That everyday expression that was so casually thrown off before it had a specific, intimate significance.

You know, everyone wants to die a normal death.

Not too soon, though. Not so quickly.

May 29, 2019
BWI Airport

When Bizu and I arrived at Baltimore airport, I went to the newsstand and got copies of The Wall Street Journal, The Washington Post, and The New York Times. We read obituaries, passing papers from hand to hand.

The Journal's obituary said Tony was "among the most talented and dogged reporters on the staff...an amiable genius—the best combination of bulldog reporter and transcendent writer."
The Times quoted David Blight, a historian Tony venerated: "Tony created his own unique genre of history and journalism.... His search for Olmsted's journey was Tony's own brilliant mirror held up to all of us about the awful social and political successes we face now as Olmsted's epic journey showed the same for the South and the road to the Civil War."
In the Post: "He was often in situations that could be considered comical, if they weren't so dangerous. In the middle of a demonstration in Tehran, Mr. Horwitz found himself in a crowd chanting 'Death to America.' He met an English-speaking demonstrator who unexpectedly asked Mr. Horwitz about Disneyland. 'It has always been my dream,' he said, 'to go there and take my children on the tea-cup ride.' Then the protester resumed shouting 'Death to America!' Another time, Mr. Horwitz was under siege from artillery fire in a boat outside Beirut, when a fellow passenger turned to him and said, 'You are very brave. And maybe very stupid.' "

This is a comforting thing. These lengthy obituaries provide a thorough description of the work he was passionate about and striking insights into his character. There's more. He would have liked the title of the obituaries in the Vineyard's two local newspapers: Tony Horwitz, Author, Historian, Regular Island Guy.

Our neighbors' love and memories are abundant in the comments on the websites of both periodicals. His friend Andrew Denton, who accompanied him on some of the reporting for Spying on the South and makes an appearance as a sidekick in one of the funniest parts of the book, wrote a loving memoir for the Sydney Morning Herald, where he worked when we lived in Australia. Both her interview with him for Confederates in the Attic and critic Maureen Corrigan's laudatory review of Spying on the South, which had debuted the week before and was enjoyed by Tony, were rerun on NPR by Terry Gross. Jill Lepore had a keen appreciation for The New Yorker, where he temporarily worked as a staff writer. "A distinguished American historian with a singular voice, full of compassion and delight and wry observations and self-deprecating humor—layers that covered but never obscured his deep and abiding moral seriousness about the task of the historian as the conscience of a nation." Her description of him would have made him blush.

And I can still feel Tony's disapproval as I write this. Cut this, I see his terse scrawl, his pen cuts. boasting.

However, I won't. I was grateful for these obituaries even though I was depressed and sitting in the airport. They brought to my attention how much Tony had accomplished in his sixty years of life and how easily it could have ended sooner had any of the outrageous risks we took during our reporting years gone awry. I also felt sorry for everyone who had lost someone on this day, whose accomplishments, humor, and peculiarities would never be known to the public. whose sons would not be able to read about their father and understand how much everyone loved and respected him.

I decided to keep that in mind as we confront the future. I decided to be thankful.

Flinders Island

My personality is Potemkin. I'm strolling down the beach this afternoon when I think of the phrase.

A refugee from my own emotions, I have constructed a façade that I have concealed behind. Every time I leave the house, I have to exert a lot of energy to carry it about because it is heavy and intricate. Particularly throughout the past year, when I have been around the world on a book tour. On the day before my novel was published, Nathaniel remarked, "Don't die, Mum," as I was leaving for the airport to travel to Tennessee for my first event.

Tony had a more belief in Horse than I did, and it was the tour for the book. I was about to give up on the book because of the special difficulties it presented, but he persisted. Only to dedicate the book to him did I pull myself back to my desk to finish it. The book that today appears to have the potential to be the most popular among readers.

The day the novel was released, I did my first appearance on that tour at Parnassus Books in Nashville. It is a store owned by a person I love and an author I respect. I caught a glimpse of Ann Patchett at an awards ceremony where Bel Canto rightfully won and Year of Wonders was shortlisted. She came to talk to me while I signed a stack of copies of The Secret Chord, which she had selected for her First Editions book club, and we finally met in 2015 in Nashville in the back room of her bookstore. The bookstore had so many dogs that I fell in love with it right away. Ann's employees are encouraged to bring their dogs to work since, like me, she is a dog lover.

As I admired Mary Todd Lincoln, a modest little dachshund who traversed the world in a baby sling, and caressed her energetic companion Sparky, she added, "I'm one dog away from being shut down by the health department."

"So," she said. "I have no knowledge of your life. Tell me.

"Well, as you are aware, Tony Horwitz is my spouse."

"No!" she cried out. "How are you finding that?"

In literary Nashville, Tony had a considerable celebrity. White supremacists—pardon me, "heritage groups"—had interrupted his first speech there, for Confederates in the Attic, and police had been summoned. When the Black cop that showed up was called the N-word, the so-called heritage guys kind of gave the game away.

Given that Tony and I had been married for thirty-one years at that point, I gave in because our marriage was going well.

Ann reminds me of my mother because she is sarcastic and sympathetic. I convinced her to present her book Commonwealth at the book festival on Martha's Vineyard so that we could get together when it was released. She stayed with us with her husband, Karl, a Mississippi chevalier.

We now had an odd connection. Nashville was where Tony and I spent our final days together. A week into his book tour, I had joined him. When the Parnassus events manager suggested that I do an interview with him, I seized the opportunity to travel with him and get back in touch with Ann.

After that occasion, we had our last lunch together with Ann and Tony's roommate Bruce from our time as graduate students at Columbia Journalism School. Southerner Bruce had made Nashville his home, living in a house a few doors from Ann's.

The day had been beautiful. Tony had just returned from a crowded event at the Atlanta location of the Jimmy Carter Presidential Library. His work was selected by Ann for her First Editions Club, which elevates a book from the bestseller list to the runway. I sat in the rear of her store that day, talking to Ann and her wonderful employees while I pushed books to Tony for signing. Since the event was just an hour away after we finished the signing, Tony and I walked to a little pub nearby for a quiet drink and caught up on all the tiny and big things that had happened during our week apart.

Tony engaged everyone who wanted to talk by signing more books at the end of the program. Even though I was eager to get to dinner, I suppressed my excitement because I knew that Tony's talent was his ability to build relationships and his genuine interest in other people.

Following supper, we retired to our hotel and embraced the cozy affection of bodies that had known one another for a long time.

I was flying home in the morning while Tony drove to Louisville for what he already knew would be a packed house at the Filson Historical Society. He told me via email the following morning that Louisville had been a huge success, with 800 people in attendance and a lot of books signed. "The only thing that went wrong was that I forgot to turn off my phone, and it rang in the middle of a conversation in my shoulder bag in the front row. To turn it off, the sleeper had to rummage through Nicorette and bloody tissues (cutting himself shaving)." I just looked, and it looks like you're using a butt dial.")

A week prior to our most recent reunion, we had gotten together with old friends in New York City and toasted the release of his book at the Brooklyn eatery Olmsted. I had sneaked out of the hotel the following morning without waking him or saying goodbye, knowing how demanding his upcoming week would be.

However, we bid each other a good farewell in Nashville that morning. "It's unbelievable that I won't see you again for ten days." He always had a clearer calendar in his mind than I did, therefore I'm positive he stated it. However, it might have just as well been me. We both sensed it. We had never been more in love than we were that morning. We were excited about life after the book tour and all the wonderful things that would occur. After exchanging long kisses, I took a taxi to the airport.

According to one of my friends, her sister had to live with the words, "I can't believe you forgot to get gas," she said to her husband the day he passed away unexpectedly.

It's unbelievable that I won't see you again for ten days.

It's unbelievable that I won't see you ever again.

One thing I will always regret is not choosing to meet him next week in Washington. However, I am at least happy that we had that final day together and those final words.

May 29, 2019

West Tisbury

It was raining hard and cold as Bizu and I got off the ferry. This was the depressing late May reversal that is all too typical of Vineyard spring. We were picked up and driven home by Bizu's godmother, Salem. There is a little town center with a basic store, town hall, white clapboard church, and library, and we reside about twenty minutes' drive from the ferry pier. The area is made up of farms and woods. The rare Vineyard home that fulfilled Tony's insatiable need to be close to a newspaper and a cup of coffee and my desire for a country lifestyle was this historic millhouse, which we were fortunate to find. Spice filled the air throughout the house. In addition to a bowl of her tahini—the greatest tahini I've ever eaten in twenty different countries—my friend Cindy had left a casserole of cinnamon chicken. Nicki had set up a pretty table and warmed everything up after taking over our neighbors' dog-sitting duties. Bizu and I hadn't wanted to eat for three days until this lunch.

There were food offerings, flowers, and condolence cards everywhere in the kitchen. With blind canine delight, Bear and Simba, the dogs, welcomed us. Appreciative of rough, simple Labrador affection, Bizu buried his face in Bear's fur.

Nathaniel texted that a tornado had delayed his flight out of Dallas. It would arrive at the airport too late to catch the final aircraft to the island. He would have to stay overnight in Boston and wake up to catch the puddle jumper.

Bizu and I then went to bed. My bedroom was empty, and I stood at the door. It was challenging to get inside. Now it would always be vacant, just like this. I tried to remind myself that this was no different than when Tony was on tour and I had been sleeping alone. Bear had superior senses. She rushed up on the bed the moment I flipped over onto my side and turned out the lamp. Rather of resting at my feet as she always does, she pressed her long, heavy body against mine, her spine to mine. "You're not alone," she seemed to be saying.

I braced myself the following morning to listen to the numerous messages on our home phone's voicemail. Time-stamped shortly after I left the house and rushed to the ferry, the earliest was from the transplant team at George Washington Hospital, requesting permission to utilize Tony's organs.

This broke my heart. Naturally, I would have agreed. There is no doubt that Tony would have desired it. When he collapsed, he was carrying his driver's license, which showed he was an organ donor.

What was the point of asking me? What good would it do to write your request on your driver's license if it will never be honored? How come the resident didn't ask me or even mention that I would be receiving this call? What had we done to ruin someone's life and health?

When my mind was clearer later, I understood that they couldn't have recovered his essential organs. They would have been failing even before he got to the emergency room. Maybe they were able to get his corneas back. Corneas could have saved someone's life. In the crematorium, instead, there was a sizzle of moisture that vanished in an instant.

After a few days, when I wasn't so distraught and upset, I called the transplant team again and chastised them for their botched procedure. "If the situation had permitted, we can provide you with a certificate stating that he would have donated his organs. For some, that is beneficial.

With clenched teeth, I murmured, "What I would find 'helpful,' is knowing that you will make changes to ensure this doesn't happen again."

There were numerous other voicemails, of course. One was a recording from our literary agent, Kris, made shortly before we got home. In her message, she announced that Spying on the South would be included in the New York Times bestseller list. Tony's labor on tour, which included eight locations in seven days, was reflected in the list that tracked sales in the week before his death.

I gave her a call back to find out whether she believed he had any inkling this would occur. Kris remarked, "I told him I was cautiously optimistic because some of his best events came at stores that report to the Times." However, I'm not sure he actually trusted me.

As I waited in Boston for Nathaniel to board his flight to the Vineyard, I informed Bizu about the bestseller list and sent him an email with the information. He replied to my email with the following: "And here he was worried not many people would read it." It would have delighted him. Oh, Dad.

For my part, I was barely aware of my emotions. Naturally, I wanted everyone to adore and respect his final creation. However, copies of Spying on the South still make me think, "There's the book that killed Tony." The tiresome tour, the writing process made possible by drugs and alcohol, and the unrelenting strain of reporting it.

But how could it have been? That's how Tony had always been. Completely committed.

As soon as I arrived in New York in September 1982 and started interacting with my fellow Columbia Journalism School graduate students, I realized how different we were in terms of class and culture. Many of these individuals appeared to be burned out before they had even begun their jobs, and they were driven in a manner that I had never been. This group of twenty somethings were exhausted. Many of them were veterans of the battle to get admission to the top prep, the prestigious elementary, or the private preschool. More pressure to achieve extracurricular activities and get impeccable grades at every turn. Acceptance to an Ivy League university's prestigious graduate program was but another battleground in their never-ending battle.

I had such a strange experience. One buddy remarked years later, "You came to the J-School like you were going to a ball." "It surprised me that you truly thought you would like it."

I did. The scholarship had given me the chance to travel to New York and improve my reporting abilities, and I was thankful for that. Whatever my goals were, they had always been mine. Never had my parents pressured me. They were okay with whatever I did. They weren't expecting distinctions, so they were excited if I received them, and they didn't feel disappointed if I didn't meet their expectations.

With my Australian mother as a radio host and my California-born father as a singer, both came from hard, impoverished homes and had achieved some improbable early success. However, for reasons I've never understood, they had given up their glitzy careers and, apparently, any ambition long before I was even born. They had made their home in an economical area of Sydney's blue-collar district. Mom became a homemaker, while Dad became a proofreader. We never traveled, had no automobile, and most of our stuff was used.

On the other hand, Tony was from a tribe of high-achieving, wealthy people who had art on their walls, traveled overseas, and attended the top universities. It was a loving, boisterous, and humorous family, but it also had high standards. It was recognized that one must strive for perfection, put forth a lot of effort, and never give up.

When Tony and I collaborated on a story, as we frequently did when working on reporting assignments in the Middle East, I would sometimes have the audacity to propose that we take a break after exhausting days and nights of reporting. Perhaps we could even take a nap or a dip in the hotel pool before we started writing. I could have just as well proposed that we jump off the balcony. Tony was simply incapable of working at anything other than his best. It was not his disposition.

He had long been aware that this behavior could have negative effects. When he began his first journalism position at the Fort Wayne News-Sentinel in 1983, he went to see a fate teller. She reported, "I've never seen a shorter lifeline than yours." He later got a "scary revelation" after reading an article about type A personalities who die young from heart attacks and suffer from "hurry sickness." He wrote in his journal: "I have to control my fears." Once more, vistas of travel and exploration open up with G., and we need to find the time to avoid being preoccupied with our careers.

Regretfully, that thought did not last long. He was contemplating his next course of action and worrying about his career prospects within a page or two of that same journal. He never succeeded in overcoming his driven temperament and hurried illness. He didn't even slow down when we chose to have children ten years into our marriage.

Despite his best efforts. After Nathaniel was born, he left The Wall Street Journal to work as a staff writer at The New Yorker, anticipating how our lives would alter. He believed that working for a magazine would provide more freedom than being a national reporter for a daily newspaper.

In the end, it was a bad fit. He switched to a company that continuously questioned his judgment from one that had trusted it. New parenthood's inevitable insomnia was made worse by last-minute, late-night calls from a phalanx of editors. Even though he authored some noteworthy pieces, he eventually became tired of superiors asking him what the story would say before he had even covered it. As a result, he stopped writing until the morning before each publication.

Fortunately, his third novel, Confederates in the Attic, did well. We moved to Sydney in search of a less demanding life as full-time authors when he signed a contract to write Blue Latitudes, a book on Captain Cook. Nathaniel picked up an Australian accent that he carried with him for years while I began writing my first novel while he dug into the Cook archives. This was our second extended stay in Sydney together. We were more confident in our career and more comfortable in our marriage. I remember it as a beautiful age. Numerous pleasant recollections: Walking Nathaniel to kindergarten at a historic schoolhouse shaded by gum trees, where the children wore wide-brimmed cloth hats to shield them from the fierce Australian sun; spending afternoons watching him and his young companions climb over sandstone outcrops and hang from trees in the remnant of foreshore bushland that had miraculously survived in our crowded urban neighborhood. On the weekends, the three of us would travel north to my mother's home by the sea. We would eat too many roast dinners thanks to her. Following the meal, Tony would relax on her banana chair in the backyard while Mum delighted in spending time with her grandson. Compared to the States, it was a simpler, less demanding life. When we lived in Australia, we experienced a better work-life balance than our friends did.

However, I couldn't hold Tony there. He was being called to the next thing, the next siren song, even before Blue Latitudes was headed for publication. The success of Spying on the South would have satisfied his need for the next achievement, even though I'm sure he would have been happy and relieved.

Bizu and I left in the late morning to pick up Nathaniel from the small airport, which was less than fifteen minutes away from the property. I would normally have gone alone. This time, however, it seemed we both had to go. We didn't even bring it up. Bizu simply got into the vehicle.

This unsteady trio. That was how we would have to continue. In a new asymmetry, we would need to learn how to balance ourselves.

Additionally, we would all need to cease arranging the table for four.

Flinders Island

I had a nightmare last night.
I'm left viewing a movie at home by Tony. Jack and Lisa, our buddies, will be picked up by him and brought back to the house. Together, we will all watch the film. The movie is good, and I'm loving it. But eventually, I start to question what's holding them. I find out later that Bruce, our Nashville friend, has joined Tony and Jack and Lisa after they met up. Without me, they all went out and had a fantastic evening. Tony is not sorry, but I am angry. My offended feelings go unanswered by him. I know that until he apologizes, acknowledges his mistake, or stones for it in some way, I will never be able to let go of my rage. However, he dismisses it. His intransigence is beyond me. I get more irate. I say terrible things.
My anger at him is so strong it wakes me up.
The dream lingers in my mind like a soggy fog all day. Where have these harsh words and terrible sentiments originated from? I'm as exhausted as if the disagreement about the dream were true.
Something is coming to the surface. I'm not sure what it is yet. Head down against the breeze, I stroll along the shore. My spirit is not cleansed of its bitterness by the salty air. Tony is no longer with me. He has continued without me. That much is obvious. However, I am the one that continues to socialize with our former pals, enjoy nights out, and cherish the priceless moments of life. It is he who is left out. It's him who's missing. Why, therefore, am I upset with him? Not just upset, but furious to a degree I never experienced with him, not even during our most heated confrontations. I had trouble sleeping that night. I'm afraid of further unsettling dreams. I'm drifting when I suddenly wake up. Now I can see it. Kübler-Ross argues rage comes after denial.
I don't feel resentful of Tony.
Death has me in a rage.

May 31, 2019

West Tisbury

Not a single clock stops. The phone is never silenced. The pianos are still playing, and the dogs are still barking.
Wystan, an elderly poet, was unable to get the world to recognize his immense loss. I can't either. It was impossible, as much as I wanted to sit behind a yew tree and cry while wearing a black veil over my head. The modern world is a juggling performance, and if you lose your concentration and drop one of the blazing torches, the entire stage could collapse and catch fire beneath you.
Tony's Social Security number set off a series of events once the death certificate was signed. Tony was the primary cardholder, thus my credit cards froze. We paid our bills that way, so even though I didn't want to think about credit cards in my gray mist of melancholy, I had to because if I didn't start working on finding new arrangements right away, we might not have phones or lights the next month. I was aware of how fortunate I was to have the money to cover such expenses. For many people, losing a spouse also means losing the source of income. I was extremely thankful that I would not be forced into poverty. I was still furious, though, when my attempts to apply for new credit cards in my own name were denied. Since 1984, I have not maintained an independent credit history. I had to start from scratch. The credit limit on the one card for which I did eventually qualify was 10 times that of the ones that were cancelled.
After 35 years, Tony and I had established a friendly division of labor in our marriage, with each of us taking on the responsibilities for which we were qualified. I took care of the visible tasks, such cooking, gardening, and housekeeping. He took care of all the things you couldn't see, including insurance, taxes, and finances. I had the luxury of never having to think about such things at all since he did it so expertly.
Tony had briefly contemplated creating a small book titled October Eggs, a humorous look at finance, prior to starting the Olmsted project.

He didn't pursue it because he felt discussing money was too taboo. However, he proceeded to prepare a proposal. This is how it began:

Here's the sad truth. I don't garden, or golf, or play the piano, or tinker in my toolshed. Instead, when I need respite, I buy and sell stocks, junk bonds, cotton futures, emerging market debt. As a boy I collected coins and slotted them into cardboard folders. As an adult I move assets in and out of my online portfolio. It's as close as I have to a hobby.

Managing money is also my rare contribution to the household. I'm a bad cook and a bad handyman who kicks appliances when they stop working. As my sons are quick to remind me, Mom is the one who takes out the wrench or toilet plunger. But there's one realm where Dad seems apt. He pays the bills and magically multiplies our savings.

Tony's grandfather, a lawyer from New Haven, taught him how to read stock hieroglyphs. He thought taking a visiting grandson to Merrill Lynch to see the ticker was a good idea. From the stability of buy-and-hold blue chips to the thrilling riskiness of commodity futures and short selling, Tony learned a lot about investing from him. One of his grandfather's favorite theories was October Eggs.

To me, this was all nerd. The tiny house my parents worked hard to pay off the mortgage on was their only asset, and they lived paycheck to paycheck. After a brief spell covering business for The Wall Street Journal, I gained a cursory understanding of price-earnings ratios and yield curves. I happily forgot most of it when I moved to the international desk and was happy to let Tony take over. On some afternoons, he would switch the satellite radio in the car to a program where loud men quarreled over stocks. One of them struck Tony as clever, and occasionally he made the deals he recommended. I pleaded with him to change the station to All Things Considered since I detested the racket. I wish I had listened now.

Every year or so, he would show me a nice page with predominantly green statistics that showed how well the assets he had chosen for our retirement funds were performing. However, I never questioned him about his decision-making process. It was the last thing I wanted to be thinking about when he passed away, and I had no idea where those accounts were or what passwords he used to access them.

The second-to-last item, perhaps. Taxes were another fiery flame that threatened to fall to the ground. Every year, Tony received a filing extension. When the deadline finally approached in the early fall, he would become agitated and wander the house, muttering our accountant's name under his breath, frequently with profanity before it. Our accountant has been with us since the 1980s. He was an extremely peculiar man who refused to use email and maintained vampire hours. Only late at night could you talk to him on the phone. I'll call him Baffert here. He had grown more and more strange over the years. Tony started to notice mistakes. He was afraid of making a mistake that might cause a lengthy relationship with the IRS, so he had to double-check every filing.

Tony has a passion for creating lists. His to-do lists were scattered all over the house, written on pieces of cardboard or the back of old envelopes, with enthusiastic, joyous lines scribbled over the completed tasks. I came across a list one day that ended with the phrase, "Check other lists."

I discovered Tony's final list before he went on his book tour on the kitchen counter, beneath a bag of gifts of muffins. It had tasks he intended to complete as soon as he got back. Fire Baffert is the first item.

At the behest of his grandfather, a lawyer from New Haven, Tony learnt to read stock hieroglyphs. His grandfather thought that taking a visiting grandchild to Merrill Lynch to view the ticker was a fitting expedition. Tony learnt about investing from him, including the exhilarating riskiness of commodity futures and short trading, and the stability of buy-and-hold blue chips. One of his grandfather's most cherished conjectures was October Eggs.

To me, it was all nerdy. With the tiny property they fought so hard to pay off as their only asset, my parents lived paycheck to paycheck. I briefly worked as a business reporter for The Wall Street Journal, where I briefly learned about price-earnings ratios and yield curves. However, I happily forgot much of that when I moved to the international desk and was happy to let Tony take over. He would switch the satellite radio to a program where loud men debated about stocks in the car on some afternoons. Tony occasionally made the transactions he recommended because he believed one of them to be wise. I asked him to turn to All Things Considered since I detested the racket. I regret not paying attention now.

He would present me with a page of predominantly green statistics that showed the performance of the investments he had chosen for our retirement accounts once a year or so. I never did, however, ask him how he came to those conclusions. I had no idea where those accounts were or what passwords he used to access them, and I didn't want to be thinking about it when dad passed away.

or the item that comes last. Taxes were another burning torch that threatened to destroy the floor. Every year Tony had a filing extension, and when the deadline finally came around in the early fall, he would get a frantic look and go around the house whispering our accountant's name, frequently followed by profanities. Since the 1980s, we had been using the same accountant. He was an odd man who refused to use email and kept vampire hours. He was someone you could only talk to on the phone late at night.

I'll refer to him here as Baffert. He had become more eccentric over the years. Tony started to identify mistakes. Fearing an error that might cause a lengthy conflict with the IRS, he had to double-check each form.

Tony likes to make lists. I would discover his to-do lists scattered about the house, written on the back of used envelopes or pieces of cardboard, with enthusiastic, joyous lines scribbled over the completed tasks. One day, I came upon a list that ended with the phrase, "Check other list."

Upon arriving home, I discovered Tony's final list before he left on his book tour, hidden beneath a bag of gifts of muffins on the kitchen counter. Things he intended to do once he got back were listed on it. First, we have a Fire Baffert.

Flinders Island

I had to switch shacks. I packed up and moved a few miles south to a different part of the western shore since Mick, the farmer, required his home for visiting family. Although it doesn't appear to be far on the map, a rocky route swirls and turns endlessly through dense bushland as soon as I turn off the main road. With bitter fury, my tangled car squeals and creaks. It's challenging, so when the gate to the new location eventually emerges amid stands of fluffy casuarinas, I feel a sense of relief.

This new shanty is a little fancier and a little smaller, with a fairly stylish kitchen and an indoor bathroom. It's even farther away. It gives the sparse collection of houses in Killiecrankie the feel of a city. Leeka, where it is located, had a population of zero in a recent census. Some friends have questioned me if I was scared to be alone in such a remote location after I've told them about it. To be honest, I never really considered myself to be anxious. It's not like I'm a brave individual. In addition to being an anxious passenger in fast cars, I'm also afraid to swim far out from the coast in choppy waves. However, being alone never worries me—not in the city, and definitely not in the wilderness. I placed it on the same shelf of improbable dangers as getting hit by lightning or getting sucked up by quicksand.

A tiny beach is directly above the hut. One more magnificent vista. To form a protected bay, a lengthy arm of stony reef slings itself from the north. The southern end is defined by a modest swell of granite poked by caves. The hut overlooks a vast expanse of open sea to the northwest. The only thing between me and the southern Indian Ocean is one little island, low on the horizon. Beyond the granite outcrop to the east, Marshall Bay's broad, white sands curve slowly toward Wybalenna and Settlement Point in the distance. No other residence can be seen that far. Sculpted boulders break up the 140 acres of casuarina, grass trees, sedges, ribbon gums, and Tasmanian blue gums that make up the property.

The most impressive of these rises suddenly, enormously, and is taller than a four-story structure. The sheer vertical cliff on one face is as smooth as if a professional stone mason had shorn it on a plumb line. There is a rising cluster of curves on the other side. The spot where the two sides, the yin and yang of these soft and hard geometries, meet is a shallow cave. At the apex, the pink stone blends into a shape reminiscent of a pair of hands joining in prayer or a Gothic three-pointed arch.

It seems like a place of worship, undoubtedly one devoted to Mother Earth. Because the secret within is protected by softly rounded sides that resemble labial folds. I feel compelled to perform a ritual here: to honor Gaia's beauty, to make amends for our transgressions against her creation, and to offer a mother's prayer for my sons' safety.

The only sounds are the casuarinas' soft susurrus and the waves. Not to mention that the wind lessens and the white caps disappear as night falls.

I have become used to being alone.

June 2, 2019
West Tisbury

I just wanted to be alone with the boys. However, that isn't feasible. Too many friends and neighbors wanted to express their condolences and couldn't wait for the funeral services that we had scheduled for August on the Vineyard and October in Washington, DC. We would have to deal with these nice friends on multiple occasions if we didn't see them together. I couldn't go to the grocery store without getting bumped by folks who were crying in the produce section.

A gathering, a shiva of sorts, would have to take place. We made a decision Sunday night.

Tony would have been returning home from his book tour on Saturday, so I had to get through that first. He would have been ecstatic to have Bizu home from school for the summer, relieved that his travels were over, elated to have made the bestseller list, and eager for Nathaniel to return from his adventures. There would have been plenty for us to rejoice.

Rather, I allowed myself to be quietly, terribly smashed in between buying sides of smoked salmon and worried about where everyone would park the following day.

It was cold and foggy Sunday afternoon. To create a large circle beneath the old apple tree's boughs, we brought every chair out into the yard. To control the flow of people, cars, plates, glasses, and other objects, my group of female friends assembled early and created a flying wedge around me. These authors, educators, artists, and filmmakers tend to be a boisterous group. It was strange to watch them so overcome with grief, talking in low tones, stumbling over each other in my kitchen, so eager to be of assistance.

The event had a peculiar quality. a vibration that is dissonant. This lawn has hosted so many happy summer parties. Tony's love of parties led to two weddings, countless book parties, and gatherings for no other purpose. I kept seeing glimpses of him as the crowd grew, the sparkle of late-afternoon sunlight on blond hair, a turn of a shoulder. I saw Nathaniel, struggling with jet lag, relying on his partner for assistance. I observed Bizu's unexpectedly mature demeanor as he greeted friends with a courteous elegance. Knowing that I feared this as much as he did, I could see his eyes on me, eager to check on me.

I had found that removing myself from other people's cries helped me deal with my own pain the best. While some friends followed my example, others did not. The sudden arrival of Ron, the third of Tony's three roommates from Columbia Journalism School and later a colleague at The Wall Street Journal, from Boston was what rescued me. Like Tony, Ron is a natural emcee at any event and has a large personality. In the middle of all the misery, he became my pillar of support and a wonderful diversion.

Our rabbi used readings from the Psalms to start a service. "Tony would have a problem with that," she said, "because these are ancient texts that assume a God who controlled everything." Here are a few contemporary psalms. She chose poetry that was appropriate and relevant to Tony's life. I particularly recall Mary Oliver's words:

> Pay attention.
> Be astonished.
> Tell me about it.

And this one, also:
> Doesn't everything die at last, and too soon?

After that reading, we stood under the apple boughs and said kaddish.

Flinders Island

Congregatory, semiaquatic, social, monogamous, and partially migrating.

Tony may have been described by these adjectives. Indeed, according to Animalia, they are characteristics of the Cape Barren goose, Cereopsis novaehollandiae. Despite being among the rarest geese in the world, they nest in considerable numbers on Flinders Island, where they settle in the tussock grasses surrounding the shack and the island's temperate wetlands.

One of the highlights of my walks is running into them. They're funny birds, big and ungainly, pale gray with pink legs and a bright green cere on top of their beak that somehow makes them look curious. They have an unmelodic call that sounds more like a pig's grunt than any bird's song.

As far as I can tell, ornithologists have not yet determined whether the bird is more like a duck or a swan. The Australian Journal of Zoology defines it somewhat unscientifically as "a most peculiar goose of uncertain affiliations." For a long time, scientists thought Cape Barren geese were the black swan's juvenile stage. They had nearly gone extinct due to hunting by the 1950s. Birds that are easy to capture, such as the heath hen, the great auk, and the moa, have not fared well under human control. However, the creation of natural reserves like those on Flinders allowed the population to gradually recover, just in time for the Cape Barren geese.

Gaggle, plump, skein, wedge, and team are evocative names for the big groups of geese that they travel in. I value their sociability while I'm by myself.

In a gaggle, Tony was always far superior than me. I was never—and never will be—the extrovert he was, even though I was able to get over my shyness by the time I completed my degree at Sydney University. I clung to him limpet-like at parties, hiding behind his gregarious demeanor. He was a kind, gregarious host, and I loved cooking when we had guests over while he led the conversation.

He would never have been able to make Flinders Island his home. His character required a bigger canvas. He had found success with

Martha's Vineyard because of the diversified and sizable influx of summer residents, which expanded our tiny group of acquaintances from all over the world. People accustomed to cautious reverence were disarmed by Tony's genuine curiosity, readiness to ask the unguarded inquiry, and occasionally willingness to venture out on risky conversational limbs. Our circle of friends grew larger the longer we stayed on the island, until the social responsibilities of summer occasionally felt too much to handle. Sometimes, my more reserved side longed for the times we'd spent alone on the island, beachcombing or wandering through the woods.

Since Tony passed away, I have struggled to maintain the same degree of sociability from our previous life together over the summers. The gaggles of Cape Barren geese remind me how much I miss Tony's hosting prowess. I have tried to carry on, remembering how I used to love feeding a large crowd around my table.

But the gaggles won't be the same without him.

June 3, 2019
West Tisbury

George, our family lawyer, lives nearby. He sent a sincere condolence note and is more knowledgeable about loss than anyone should be.
Nathaniel and I drove the short distance to his office on the Monday morning following the Shiva to find out what we needed to do next in this obstacle course to legally end a life.
In 2008, shortly after Tony and I returned from Ethiopia with Bizu, George had drafted fresh wills for us. Nathaniel and I got down at his gleaming conference table eleven years later and went over the lengthy material. I had forgotten how complicated it was.
Tony and I had made basic wills when we were married. Since we didn't have much back then, we each created a one-page document, leaving the other to handle it. It had seemed wise to update these after we had purchased a home, welcomed Nathaniel into our family, and adopted Bizu.
I hadn't given that task my full attention. I was still sorting through the deluge of documents related to Bizu's adoption. After we got him home, we had to reapply for adoption under US law in the Dukes County courthouse, even though we had already done it legally under Ethiopian law. I was tired of legalese and much more concerned with settling a cautious child into our family than I was with going over wills. I was completely unaware of the discussions Tony and George were having regarding potential modifications to the estate tax legislation, Massachusetts and federal regulations, marital trusts, and residual trusts. Tony was an expert in trusts and taxes. Even though I read the roughly thirty pages of my updated will, which was exactly like Tony's, it didn't dawn on me that what we were building was a complex structure that was not justified by the extent of our possessions or our straightforward desires.
I was going to suffer for my lack of focus now.

This elegant document was more intricate than the typical Vineyarders' wills, which are filed throughout the year. The local probate court clerk was new to the position and wary. She had told the judge that the will could not be probated until a guardian ad litem was appointed to safeguard the interests of Bizu, a juvenile, since she was anxious about the consequences of the will.

The concept of guardians ad litem was unfamiliar to me. These are appointed in cases of contested wills, family dysfunction, contentious divorces, and egregious incompetence, according to a brief internet search.

We were exempt from all that. The court's attempt to infringe on my parental rights in this manner astounded me. How could they imply that Bizu's mother, me, was unreliable in looking out for his best interests? Together, Tony and I had accumulated the assets listed in the will. It was infuriating to have a stranger designated by the court oversee my agency's decision regarding their disposition. How the law treats a capable surviving parent is unthinkable.

I informed George that I would fight this in court and would not consent to it. I didn't want to think about it any more, and it was another distraction from the grieving process. I thought I had no other option.

My workplace was no longer familiar. When we relocated to London from Cairo to a little terrace house in Hampstead from the eighteenth century, we purchased the thin walnut tavern table. Although we hadn't had much time for domesticity because of the Gulf War and other emergencies we had been called out to cover, it had been our dining table. Our duffel bags were half-packed in the closet throughout those years, including the necessary items for international correspondence, such as field dressings, shortwave radios, bricks of cash for nations that did refuse cards, my chador, and a ballistic vest. A library table that could accommodate twenty people replaced the little tavern table in the dining room as our lifestyles changed and we had more time for dinner gatherings.

Instead of legal papers, financial spreadsheets, and baskets of condolence messages, I was accustomed to seeing my desk cluttered with notes for my fiction. I answered each of these notes myself for about a week. There were hundreds by the second week. In the end, I hired a friend's daughter to address envelopes for the replies and photocopied a sincere thank-you note. I appreciated these messages, particularly the ones that told me a little-known story about Tony. They overwhelmed me, too. I felt chastised by the pile as they continued to arrive, accumulating unchecked on my desk as I attended to every financial and legal necessity instead. I thought friends would pardon me for not answering them at last. I would drag myself into my study to look at the newest stack of papers and question whether I would ever be creative again.

I was about to get buried by papers when my sister from Australia showed up. Throughout our adult lives, we had supported one another during challenging times. Darleen frequently flew to the Vineyard to support me during my mother's several medical crises once her health started to deteriorate and she moved in with me. She now dragged me away from my desk, the confusing numbers, and the angry legal filings. She brewed strong, hot Australian tea. Breathing in the lovely late-spring air, we strolled along the beaches. I felt free to go out on my daily errands with her by my side, where islanders, quiet New Englanders, offered their sympathies in the form of unspoken hugs or parcels of fresh fish for which they would take no cash.

Even though I wasn't in a good enough state to make them, there were decisions that needed to be made. I was embarrassed to ask people to attest to my competence to care for my child, so I had to collect affidavits for the motion to waive the guardian appointment. I waited for a court date in front of the busy traveling judge who only visited the island twice a month once all the documentation was filed. My lawyer and I walked past bright clapboard homes with their picket fences tangled with blooming hydrangeas and roses to the Edgartown courthouse when our case finally made it onto his calendar. It was my turn to be heard after we waited through case after horrible case in the dismal courtroom of dysfunction, family tragedy, and feuding.

I believed that the last atrocity in this harsh bureaucracy of death was having to defend my right to mother my own son in court.

However, I was mistaken about that.

Flinders Island

granite that is porphyritic. coarse gravel. soils that are high in silica. sedimentary sequences that are folded. sharp, worn siltstone chunks that have been honeycombed by the sea and wind. large phenocrysts of K-feldspar. xenoliths of basalt. The Upper Devonian Blue Tier Batholith.

Nothing puts you in perspective like a geological timeline.

Flinders and the other islands in the Bass Strait are all that remain of the land bridge that connected Tasmania with the Australian mainland when the seas rose between 12,000 and 18,000 years ago. In terms of human generations, 18,000 years is not that long ago. About seven hundred generations have lived and passed away since this island became an island, if there are four generations every century and forty every thousand years. Every generational death, I attempt to picture who was grieving and who was grieving. Was the sorrow of loss lessened when early death was common, or did each loss become even more agonizing due to life's precarity?

The rocks are asking these questions. The rocky granite mountain range makes about one-third of this island. I had no idea this everyday rock could be so diverse and exquisite. I picture the blistering ash, the acrid fumes, the cracking and hissing as solid earth is driven through a liquid ocean, the molten ores, the searing heat, and the seething earth that gave origin to these rocks. Disarray and noise gradually give way to solidity and quiet.

There are some books about the island's natural history in the shack, and I go through the geology chapters, diving into jargon I don't know. The Germans first used the phrase "batholith," which comes from the Greek words for "depth" and "stone," in the early 20th century. English, that promiscuous word-borrower, quickly adopted it. Another Greek word for phenocryst is phaneros, which means "conspicuous, shining," and kristallos, which means "gem." Five times larger than the surrounding crystals in the rock, phenocrysts are showpieces. Do diamonds have phenocryst properties? My research reveals that the answer is no. They are foreign diamonds called xenocrysts that have been torn from the edges of the magma pipes that are rushing up through the crust and carried up from the earth's mantle.

I wore a diamond ring that had belonged to Tony's great-grandmother, Bubbe Rose, when we married. An engagement ring had been missing. No more than I wanted the other pricey accoutrements of the wedding-industrial complex, I didn't want one. I purchased a cheap off-the-rack ensemble consisting of a lace slip dress and a white angora jumper. At her house on a French hill, my sister and I handled all the cooking. The mayor of the sixteenth-century local town hall married us to obey secular French law, then a rabbi remarried us in my sister's garden, surrounded by brooms and lavender, with only fifteen guests. The chuppah was a tallit that was strung on doweling that we had purchased the previous day from the neighborhood bricolage. My toes were pinched all day because I had neglected to pack nice shoes, which I also had to buy at the last minute.

However, wearing that elegant diamond ring in its vintage platinum setting made me happy. I received it from Tony's mother, Ellie, just before the wedding. It meant that I had been accepted into a family of women who had persevered, survived, and thrived in the face of overwhelming adversity: immigrants, matriarchs, survivors of exile and pogrom.

Ellie read a poem she had written during the wedding feast. Ellie, a well-known author of children's and young adult books, was known for her humorous "occasional poems" at family get-togethers, and this one emphasized how unlikely our union was:

If in Sydney you start to dig
Into the earth at a steady pace
A trillion zillion miles away
You'll come up in Chevy Chase.
If in Maryland you begin
To search the world both far and near

Once you've covered terra cognita
You'll find there's a whole other hemisphere!

The odds of us meeting had been absurdly long, as Ellie noted. It had taken place during the first week of graduate school on a Manhattan balcony during a party hosted by a classmate. At that time, Alphabet City was a difficult part of the Lower East Side. Tony, a tanned, tousle-haired blond in overalls and red sneakers, regaled the small gathering on the balcony with the miseries of living with his brother. He had discovered that the local criminals had a little con: they would take the battery out of your car and resell it to you from the local used car parts shop. Before realizing that he needed to bring both the battery and the car key when he parked, he had already bought his battery back twice. I saw the funny blond across the room the following day as the class assembled in Columbia's World Room for the dean's formal welcome. I gave a wave. He didn't return the wave. I didn't think about him again for the remainder of the semester after thinking, "That's rude."

We discovered during winter break that we had both impulsively enrolled in the business reporting course. We all reasoned that if we wanted to report on capitalism's excesses and shortcomings, we needed some skills to analyze it.

His idealism and, to be honest, his well-defined forearms drew my attention in class. After working as a union organizer in Meridian, Mississippi, where he was attempting to secure equitable compensation for low-income Black woodcutters, he traveled to journalism school. He and Josh had returned there over spring break to work on a documentary called Mississippi Wood, which would eventually be broadcast on PBS. I noticed that his arms were aesthetically tanned a rich hazelnut, with his shirt sleeves pushed up. After a spring break trip to the Soviet Union for young journalists, I was as pale as a bedsheet.

As we got to know one another, I found out that he hadn't waved back to me in the World Room that morning because he couldn't even see me because he had lost his spectacles down the toilet at Danceteria while celebrating with his brother the previous evening. He was later deterred from approaching me after noticing that I was always seated with a dashing student called Bronstein at seminars, leading him to believe that we were in a romantic relationship. I had to let him know that the seminar's seating was arranged alphabetically by last name.

Our first kiss under the ugly bridges over Amsterdam Avenue during the final week of classes was a major turning point in our relationship. Since he was going to an internship on the West Coast and I had already accepted a position in The Wall Street Journal's Cleveland bureau, this was not the best time to start a new relationship. It appeared like our relationship would only be a short-lived flirtation in graduate school.

But he spent the weekend in Cleveland visiting me on his way west. The Journal had booked me into a hotel in the heart of the city while I was looking for an apartment. After Tony left on Monday, I came back from work to see a hand-pieced blanket created out of work shirts and sugar sacks that Tony had purchased in Mississippi, adding some color to the otherwise drab décor of my hotel room. Just a few miles outside Cleveland, Tony's car radio died as he was heading west. He had nothing to do but reflect on the amazing time we had just had during the entire journey across the nation. He turned and returned weeks later. The closest reporting position he could find was as an education reporter for the Fort Wayne News-Sentinel, which was four hours away from Cleveland. We spent our days off together, taking turns traveling through blizzards on Friday nights. At my sister's home in the Alpes-Maritimes, where we were married a year and a half later, Tony's mother read her poem about how this unexpected romance had triumphed over all odds.

June 16, 2019
West Tisbury

The historian Tony had a fondness for cemeteries. He had rubbed the grim old Puritan death heads that adorn so many New England gravestones as a child. But he would have no grave, stone or memorial. He had never liked to discuss death.

I was a strong advocate of advance directives because I had taken care of my mother during the protracted theft of Alzheimer's disease and was clear about the type of end-of-life experience I did not desire. Tony would not participate in these discussions. He would quickly leave the room after discovering an urgent task that he had to complete immediately. He didn't want to consider his own potential future illness or our aging. He didn't have to, as it turned out.

His only statement was that he wanted his ashes interred in his baseball mitt at the dirty Chilmark field, where he used to play softball on Sunday mornings during the summer. This may have been a casual comment, but the boys and I agreed to follow it because it was the only directive we had.

He adored the strange variety of island folks that attended that softball game. He would bring me coffee and the New York Times every Sunday before rushing off to be present for "mitts in," the custom in which players would toss their gloves into a pile and the league's "commissioners" would alternately pick them up, randomly filling out club rosters. The game had a lengthy history and its own whimsical set of rules. Because it was on the road, a ball that struck as far as the dirt track near the field's edge was referred to as a Kerouac. No one was supposed to dive in to collect a ball that fell in the poison ivy patch, therefore it was considered a homer. Bizu took Tony to Little League games when he was eight and played pinch runner for some of the older, arthritic players. Tony was thrilled to win Rookie of the Year at the end of the season.

Following each game, Tony would write outrageous "after-action reports" that were full of ludicrous fabrications about the play of the morning while giggling to himself. One player, Jerry, had a knee replacement, but Tony exaggerated the process into a fake set of procedures that made Jerry completely bionic. He started using inverted commas to allude to him.

In a customary letter to his teammates, he said, "Labour Day at Flanders Field is always bittersweet and was especially so this year due to the tragic quality of the play." A rare mental blunder by "Jerry," who was speeding toward third, which was already occupied by a teammate, was one of the bonehead actions. After being tagged out, he stated, "That's why I'm having my next surgery tomorrow." The term artificial intelligence

Another player, well-known for his staunch support of the Israeli right, was also frequently made fun of. Joel G. showed off his rippling Aipac after intense training with the Judea and Samaria League by lifting his shirt. Then, while trash-talking and flashing some great leather, he applied a Philadelphia tag to my solar plexus with such force that I gasped. "Take that, you raghead-loving, running-dog J-Streeter!" he exclaimed with delight. """ The teammates took pleasure in the jokes and gave Tony a special Fake News Award, complete with a trophy of its own.

His ashes were prepared for an eco-burial and received in a lovely handmade paper container embellished with pressed ferns and wildflower seeds.

In the box containing our sporting equipment, I discovered his lefty mitt. As he ran backward, squinting into the sun and grabbing for a long fly ball, I thought of the excitement on his face as I pressed it to my face and smelled the leather and sweat. After I selected some native columbines, we went to the field to grant his wishes.

It's a shabby field across from the Chilmark town landfill on a dirt road. However, it is encircled by woods, and on a windy day, the branches gently whisper in the air. In an effort to cause as little disruption to the field as possible before Opening Day this summer, I carefully pulled out a square of sod and then had the boys dig the hole. I placed the flowers on top when we swapped out the sod. We hugged and cried as we stood next to this strange grave. Father's Day was that day.

The blooms would be blown away by the wind that night, and by the following summer, it would be hard to tell where we had dug. Only the recollections of the wonderful moments and laughter from those Sunday mornings when he had been content would serve as his memorial.
These lines were later included in a poem my sister wrote:

There he rests in a cradle of a hand
Cushioned in familiar folds of skin that he once held
Together they leapt into the light
Catching and returning with speed
Caps off as you pass that field
It holds treasure in it.

Flinders Island

The terrace in front of the shack has a dead bird on it. With a piece of prey still securely clasped in its beak, it lies flawless and bloodless.

It had to have struck the sliding door's glass. Humans are usually deadly to other animals.

It's a recent death. The bird's spherical eye has a black glow. Ants still haven't discovered it. I picked up the small body. I can fit it in my hand's palm. The wings and back have warm russet feathers, while the breast is decorated with tan and white scallops. The tail is long and lanky. I don't recognize the bird, and the hut doesn't have any birding literature. The brown thornbill is the closest match I can locate later, after I get access to a field book.

I carefully set it on a bed of casuarina fronds that had fallen, after carrying it out to the trees. The morsel that is stubbornly stuck in its beak looks like a spider leg. The bird probably wasn't carrying the spider to nestlings at this late in the summer. Before its abrupt conclusion, I hope it had a good last meal.

I notice movement as I make my way to the beach the next morning. There is a fluttering bird. I believe it was simply stunned and is now recovering since reasoning fails me for a second. However, as I get closer, I can tell that the bird does not possess vitality. It is the frantic activity of maggots as they feast. All a-ripple with the undulations of innumerable worms hidden beneath its feathers, the thornbill writhes and twitches. These hungry hordes are efficient. After a day, not much is left. A scatter of bare bones, a fleshless tangle of feathers.

It ought to be a disgusting sight, yet it comforts me: this bird, which ended unexpectedly with a half-eaten meal, now eaten in a wild jitterbug.

I hope my own demise comes unexpectedly. Don't put me in the crematorium. Drop me directly into the ground. I would like to participate in this dance.

June 20, 2019

West Tisbury

Buffet fire.

Above a series of more readily actionable items, such as Julia Graduation Gift and Pick Up Mower, were the words of Tony's post-book tour to-do list.

Buffet fire. I gazed at his penmanship. The directive was clear-cut. But how? I can't fire our thirty-year accountant, but Tony could. I am not well-informed. When I previously filed my taxes, the employer withheld my taxes because I was a rookie reporter at The Wall Street Journal's Cleveland bureau. We've been working for ourselves for decades, and I have no idea how it's worked. It wasn't until I was hit with a penalty that I realized I had already missed the June installment, therefore I had no idea about projected taxes. When I had called Baffert to inquire about possible tasks, he hadn't considered telling me about it.

I didn't shoot Baffert.

For the management of my accountant, I engaged an accountant. To give Baffert a workable order, I gave her all the folders of receipts and statements I had discovered in Tony's study. And it was her responsibility to spot any mistakes he made.

I also hired a financial advisor. He examined the structure of investments Tony had made to fortify our future, scowled at the cryptocurrency, stared at the Chinese equities ("China is too opaque"), and suggested that I sell those holdings and exchange them for bonds. I could practically hear Tony snoozing at the prospect of dull AAAs and low-risk munis.

The advisor said, "I think you're going to be fine as long as you can continue writing and don't suddenly feel the need to purchase a private jet."

Write more. And there was the catch. Until I turned in a completed manuscript of Horse, I would not get paid.

I had no idea how I was going to end it. Since Tony's passing, I hadn't added a single word to the story and was barely halfway through. Since the day I had called and found out he was gone, I hadn't even accessed the file on my computer. The task was not feasible.

A wombat-hole immersion is necessary while writing fiction. There is only the unspooling story and you when you descend into that dim, cramped space. Court motions, tax filings, memorial plans, and responses to condolence notes were all out of the question down there. Furthermore, there was no room for the beast of anguish to cling to me with its claws as unyielding as fish hooks

Flinders Island

.Tony had kept a notebook for years before he began writing books full-time. Some years were spent in shabby spiral notebooks, while others were spent in elegant leather bound journals. Except for one explosive event early in our courtship, I had never infringed upon his private thoughts.

I'll read them now. His papers are wanted by Columbia University. An archivist who visited the residence and prepared them for delivery to Butler Library has already sorted them into boxes.

My sister, a biographer, has advised me to review everything before sending it off. She had experienced deeply personal insights when sitting in archives on multiple occasions that she believed were inappropriate for a stranger to see. I don't know how Tony would feel about every thought found in these many boxes, but he loved digging deep into archives. I have a strong suspicion that he would rather his papers remain unfiltered, regardless of what they may disclose. But before I send them off, I do want to spend some time alone with his thoughts.

Four of his journals, chosen at random from one of the crates, are with me. I sit on the deck and start thinking back on our lives.

I began at Columbia because I happened to have taken out the journal from the year we first met. My sister's statement regarding "intimate revelations" immediately makes sense to me. He had come to Columbia as he was slowly and pathetically pulling himself out of a fatal but intense college affair. Apparently sleeping with quite a few of our Columbia classmates was a necessary component of moving on from it during the fall semester.

As the list gets longer, I laugh in awe: And her? Of all people, not her? I then move on to the December 31, 1982 entry. At that point, he and I had not yet begun taking the business reporting course together, and we were halfway through journalism school. He resolves to approach his writing "NOT as a mood activity, but as work to be done each and every day" in the new year. It has been a while since my writing felt fluid in that way, but I hope to recapture it sometime this spring and show off my talent. Sure, you might write better on a Saturday night when you're stoned, but it's the weekday mornings of throwaways that make those moments of inspiration fluid. What else is there to do in the new year? 1983. A meaningless number, no resonance at all. Nothing. Allow it to happen.

Naturally, we are the ones who arrive. It is unlucky that I make my first appearance in this story toward the end of March. It had been a dismal day for him. He had been sick, there had been huge lines at the student medical center, and he had gotten into a fight with one of his casual lovers, who threw a beer in his face and told him she hated him. He owed me a bottle of champagne as it seemed we had bet on something and I had won. "It's alright if you get drunk on champagne with Geraldine," he writes. I only make another appearance as a comforting figure in May, right before the end of the school year. Someone else received the traveling scholarship he had intended to win. "I won't talk about it any more after this, but that was dumb," Geraldine said to me in the restaurant tonight. She is always so wise, but let it all go, and I will. There is no justice in it. In addition, there is some intimacy that hasn't been seen in a long time. Is it only her intelligence, cunning, and blue eyes?

He recently relocated to Fort Wayne to be close to me by the conclusion of this journal. Our connection is well-established and committed. I would like to hear him recount our story, but it will have to wait. For not bringing consecutive journals, I despise myself. December 1985 is the start of the next one I have. We've been married for two years. Following our wedding, we relocated to Sydney. I wanted to be home to help my mother and spend time with my father, who was dying of emphysema. It had been my hope that Tony would adore Sydney and that we would establish a life there.

It appeared promising. He was employed by The Sydney Morning Herald even before his jet lag subsided. He had found a niche for entrepreneurial writing in Fort Wayne, but he still had to cover school boards and perform all the other duties of a beat writer. The Herald soon trusted his gut and let him pick his own stories, even wild ones like mailing back dispatches and riding across the Outback. It became a humorous and insightful series on the Australian character. Tony got a letter shortly after the last installment:

Dear Mr Horwitz,
For some time now I have been an admirer of your writing in the Sydney Morning Herald. Should you wish to pursue any particular topic in greater depth, i.e. a book, I would love the opportunity to discuss it with you.

The book, One for the Road: A Hitchhiker's Outback, was released in Australia in 1987 and picked up in the US the following year for Random House's renowned travel line, Vintage Departures. The author was editor of Harper & Row. This excited Tony, and as he got into the project, he realized that writing books instead of everyday journalism might be his true vocation. When he broached the idea with his father by phone, he received little encouragement. According to his father, "this family has twenty books and nothing to show for it." It was with a laugh that Tony told me the comment. He was yet restless due to the demand for traditional "success." "It is perhaps telling that this morning I reached the last sentence of the book, and tonight I type out a letter to the Wash. Post—already, compulsively, on to the next thing," he wrote in his journal on New Year's Eve 1986.
It came out that the Washington Post was still uninterested. One editor remarked, "We're top heavy with white Jewish males." Another said, "Compared to applicants we've been following for a few years, you represent a risk." You wouldn't want this job, according to Newsday. even if it were yours. which I doubt you will do.")
Tony poured himself into his work as a Herald writer, penning outstanding features and pieces that made the front page. We were relaxing on the couch watching a DVD of Three Days of the Condor one evening in early May 1987, right after dinner, when the phone

rang. Tony groaned and said, "You don't have to answer it." However, I was concerned about my father's health. I pulled myself out from beneath his arm, thinking it might be a call from my mother. He was foreign editor for The Wall Street Journal. This was concerning. She hadn't called in the two years I'd been working for her. In my last story, I discussed how climate scientists in New Zealand were examining sheep methane emissions. Was I going to receive criticism for using too many jokes about farting sheep in The Wall Street Journal?

Tony had gone to the restroom and paused the video. I told him, "Well, the Middle East would be great," when he returned.

My previous Journal career wasn't really equipped for a position of that magnitude, which involved covering basic industry in Cleveland and traveling throughout Australia to write colorful articles about Outback cattle drovers and barge captains transporting supplies to isolated Aboriginal towns. However, Tony found the offer's high risk/high reward aspect intriguing: As a Mideast journalist, I would cover twenty-two nations from my headquarters in Cairo. He often worked as a freelancer for the paper, with the prospect of a staff post in the future. After playing a mind game, we discovered that neither of us could correctly identify the prime minister of Israel or the leader of any Arab state. Did Sudan rank higher or lower than Ethiopia? With our little knowledge, we had no right to accept the position.

Nevertheless, we managed to make it work after moving to Cairo. In addition to the Journal, Tony wrote for numerous other publications, such as Harper's, The Dallas Morning News, and The Courier-Journal (Louisville). He wrote fifty-six stories for ten different periodicals in the ten months after arrival. He had the experiences, but I had the steady income and the prestigious title. I had to keep up with the must-have stories about head-of-state interviews and Arab summits. He rode into the desert with the last Egyptian Camel Transport Corps or grabbed a ride on a Goan dhow navigating the mine-strewn waters of the Persian Gulf, while I sat in the luxurious salons of ministerial offices being misled.

He was given a second book contract to write Baghdad without a Map, a memoir about the Middle East that reflected our divided professional lives. He wrote of being invited to chew qat in a traditional Sufi healer's mud-brick house in Yemen. Mansour switched on the television news without making any noise as he leaned back on pillows and grew intoxicated in a room with alabaster and stained glass windows. The screen displayed a Western woman interviewing Yemen's president while holding a pad and pen. I was shocked at the picture. Geraldine was exactly like that. Then I understood that wasn't a qat delusion, but Geraldine. She was moving forward with her itinerary, which pleased me. I chewed at a final green sprig of qat and sank further down the pillow to finish my.

The long-desired staff position had not yet been filled two years after that trip to Yemen. He remained a stringer and gloomy about his future. He wrote, "It seems very remote now that I shall ever really amount to something in journalism," while he was by himself in Cairo on February 27, 1989.

I'm laughing so hard as I read this by myself on the terrace. As the new star reporter in The Wall Street Journal's London desk, he would be avoiding rifle fire on Timișoara's streets by Christmas of that year while covering Romania's revolution. Soon later, we would both return to the Middle East and take the lead in covering the first Gulf War for the paper. As the first American journalist to enter Kuwait City with the liberating soldiers, Tony would win the contest. For our coverage of the war, we would both get an Overseas Press Club Award. He would go on to win the Pulitzer Prize for National Reporting four years later for his Journal series "9 to Nowhere," which focused on low-wage labor in America.

I just so happened to pack his journal for the year he received the Pulitzer Prize. He talks with old-guard greats like Shelby Coffey, Seymour Topping, and Fred Friendly over "wine and salmon and a few words from Peter Kann, standard stuff about how this will follow us to the obituary page." He also describes how he feels "the establishment embraced" after receiving the prize in New York. The metal detector at the airport is then activated by the leaded crystal trophy that bears Joseph Pulitzer's head. The security officer doesn't even bother to look at it when I remove it from the bubble wrap. Who cares about your damn trophy, you schmuck? Get back to reality!

However, he was content at that meal, looking dapper in the same wheat-colored linen suit he had worn to our wedding (since he rarely needed a suit for his work, it hadn't seen much wear), and his parents were ecstatic at his accomplishment.

What a waste of never achieving anything in journalism.

Even while I think it's humorous, I'm a little sad to hear that he struggled with such crippling insecurities. He hadn't expressed his dejection. Generally speaking, these journals are not enjoyable to read. Seldom do I find my cheerful, humorous lover in these pages. When he wasn't that guy—that guy didn't need them—I started to see that he resorted to his writings. According to French novelist Henry de Montherlant, "happiness writes white" because it is difficult to write on paper. The pen can more easily poke dark thoughts, worries, and the insecure ramblings of insomniac nights, and the ink can drip more easily and be more readable. I am so relieved and delighted to see that: "Our marriage remains the one thing that I feel is completely mine, made of clean cloth, free of any impurity that makes me uneasy, my haven." God knows, I'm quite sure of nothing but her these days, and I wish I knew how to adequately convey how much I love her.

And I wish I could tell him his expression was perfectly OK.

I set the diaries down and go for a walk, reflecting on how little we can predict about the future and worrying that the Tony of 1989 was unaware of how successful and brilliant his career was about to become.

I realize the consequence as I kick at the sand.

I'm glad the Tony of 2019 didn't realize that his future was going to suddenly disappear on a street corner as he fell into the dark. Both the sparkling award and the unexpected death are possibilities that we are aware of. The former is what we think. The latter is rejected by most of us. Even if it confronts us, deny it.

Three months before his death, on a cold evening, Tony entered the kitchen with a distressed expression. An unexpected heart attack had claimed the life of Lincoln, one of his closest boyhood friends and a professor of art in Washington, DC. "He simply passed away at the age of sixty." I gave Tony a hug while he ran a hand over his hair. I felt it was odd that someone would die so young and so abruptly. How terrible for his wife and children. I failed to see how we would be affected by this news. I didn't think I could be that wife; Tony could be Lincoln.
What caused my blindness?

June 26, 2019
West Tisbury

Our health insurance was discontinued.

The duty of modifying our policy to cover three of us rather than four was the last chore I had to complete on the list of necessary tasks. After placing me on hold, the customer support representative returned to inform me that, as of May 28, the day following Tony's passing, my insurance had been discontinued. The children and I had been without insurance for a month in the potentially disastrous American health care system as he was the major policyholder. Until I applied for a completely new policy, which could take weeks, we would stay that way.

The outrageous amount that self-employed people must pay to properly support a family is about $5,000, which I had already paid to cover us that month. In reality, we had not purchased anything with that money. She promised to restore the money eventually, but not to my account where it had been taken out. I wouldn't see it again until after probate since it would be returned to my husband's estate.

Is this correct? Is it legal? Undoubtedly, widows and orphans shouldn't have their health insurance abruptly terminated. I was trembling with fear and rage as I hung up the phone. What if one of us died before I had a chance to resolve this? Even though these youngsters were completely dependent on me now, I had unintentionally put them—and we all —in danger.

Australians find it difficult to comprehend the unfairness of the US healthcare system because everyone is covered by taxpayer-funded Medicare, a concept that is shared by both the left and the right. Australians are shocked to hear how disease drives Americans to bankruptcy and how the uninsured may have to pay tens of thousands of dollars annually for life-saving drugs. This lunacy had made me numb. But it was insane to think that someone could spend nearly $5,000 on insurance for a month and still be uninsured.

You are aware of privilege during a crisis. During his undergraduate summer, Nathaniel worked as an intern for our Massachusetts senator, Ed Markey, who supported the Affordable Care Act. Experts on the complexities of America's dysfunctional healthcare system composed Markey's senior staff. After sending me an email and following up with a call, a senior executive from the insurance company called me two days later to reassure me that our coverage will be restored.

I was fortunate to be able to resolve the issue so rapidly after I identified it. What about everyone who didn't have a senator's office at their fingertips? Senator Markey's staffer informed me, "We are going through the wording of the Affordable Care Act to see how this was even possible and what we need to do to fix it." Who might not have even realized they were uninsured until their child had a catastrophic accident or the pharmacy charged them hundreds or even thousands for their life-saving medication?

Flinders Island

Light leaves the sky at a slow pace in this deep latitude, although summer is almost over. I'm cooking on a grill outdoors on the shack's deck when the sky is still cobalt and the horizon is still orange. In the shade of the tree line, the timid wallabies who pass by at sunset have collected. Their shadows are barely visible to me, curled like the capital L of a calligrapher.
Two of my friends come, their expressions solemn. How did they end up here?
One reaches over and rubs my shoulder tenderly. "We've come here to tell you that you wished someone had been with you the last time."
A great fear. My heart is racing when I wake up.
The abrupt precarity of my life is reflected in the nightmare.
There is no way I can afford to lose anyone else.

June 27, 2019
West Tisbury

And finally, exactly one month after his death, the autopsy report arrived.

It was a relentless inventory of Tony's beloved body, reduced to its parts. Heart valves, kidney capsules, lung lobes, genitalia, described as "unremarkable." (Well, not to me, doctor.)

Josh and I flinched our way through it, Josh writing to say that he had been driven by the medicalized jargon to the refuge of his poetry books. He had landed on Yeats:

Consume my heart away; sick with desire

And fastened to a dying animal

We found out that high blood pressure and vascular disease were major factors in Tony's death, which was attributed to "a myocarditis event." "A lengthy word at the heart of his heart." A long word is killing him. In Brideshead Revisited, Cara, the mistress of Lord Marchmain, tells Charles Ryder this.

heart disease. It's not a very long word. But I was unaware of it in June 2019. We've all heard of myocarditis since COVID. Doctors and school nurses became aware of its symptoms when it appeared as a rare side effect of the COVID immunization, particularly in young males.

After consulting with the medical examiner, Tony's cardiologist called me to discuss the results.

Tony's myocardium, the muscular center of his heart, had been infected and inflamed during the months of April and May. That's why he was out of breath when he played tennis and rushed for that train. Either the inflammation or the scar tissue it had produced moved to a location in the myocardium late on May 27th, disrupting the intricate and sensitive electrical signaling system that causes the heart to beat. The arrhythmia proved to be lethal.

The doctor asked me if Tony had the virus earlier this year. I was unable to think of one. He clarified that a viral infection is the most prevalent cause of myocarditis, which could be as minor as a head cold. Only a post mortem reveals the scars it leaves behind, and about one-third of people recover without realizing they had it. Another third will get worse over time and might require various treatments, including a heart transplant. Like Tony, the last third will pass unexpectedly. The heart fails to pump blood to the brain because it is trembling. Permanent brain damage begins in four minutes without blood or oxygen, possibly even before Mr. Ryan saw Tony lying prone on Northampton Street. Death is only five minutes away. Before the two ambulances arrived, Tony was probably already dead.

Males are twice as likely as females to have myocarditis, which commonly affects young, healthy, athletic individuals. Despite being considered uncommon, it ranks as the third most common cause of unexpected death for children and young people.

The Myocarditis Foundation states that exhaustion and shortness of breath are possible symptoms, if any exist. "Preventing more cardiac injury can be achieved by avoiding prolonged, intense exercise. Competitive sports and strenuous exercise should be avoided. Alcohol can damage an already compromised heart and raise the risk of arrhythmias, especially when consumed in excess. Products with caffeine should be avoided.

Tony's poor, ailing heart had been suffering from everything he had been doing, even the ostensibly healthy activities like regular, intense exercise.

I started to reevaluate my assumptions on his passing. This was not a clear-sky lightning strike. He hadn't been a man in excellent health who suddenly passed away. He had been ill. At least two months had passed since he began to slowly die. In our bed, dying with his arm thrown over me. He was dying as he trudged to and from his study in the barn, leaving a mark on the grass. dying at the YMCA on the StairMaster.

I knew Tony had been open about his habits from his medical records and the emails he and his doctor exchanged. These included his unhealthy alcohol use and his off-label use of Provigil, a medication that sharply improves concentration but raises blood pressure, particularly when combined with Nicotine and caffeine, which the doctor knew Tony also overused. He had given him advice on how to cut back on his drinking; they spoke on the phone frequently and it was working, albeit slowly.

I ought to have done more. I now wish I had been a typical harridan, a nagging wife who gave orders about bad behaviors. At the end of the day, I was the one who made it possible, gleefully pouring wine into his glass. I hadn't given the drinking enough thought, and I hadn't given him enough thought. I knew that Tony had sought advice from friends who had embraced sobriety. He wanted confirmation that they were still having fun and needed to know what their lives were like after drinking. One of these pals told me, "I was dismissive at first when Tony called." "You're a Jew; Jews don't drink," I told him. I then inquired about his drinking habits, and, well. Whoa.

I didn't have to inquire about Tony's response. I was aware.

Nevertheless, I had persuaded myself that this was a temporary problem, one that the demands of the book had caused, and that we could readily resolve at a later time. And to be honest, I really enjoyed our wine-fueled fun together. I could have saved him time—the few weeks he needed to get to those tests that would have shown his heart's dangerous state—if I had been more aware of the harm being done, taken better care of him, and insisted on moderation. However, I cannot and will never know that.

What I do know is that the street CPR in Chevy Chase most likely never had a chance to save him. Few people who collapse with ventricular fibrillation return via CPR, despite what TV dramas portray, unless they are at a hospital with a crash cart and a code team. The New England Journal of Medicine reports that the chances of a revival are less than 5% of the 356,000 cardiac arrests that occur outside of hospitals in the US each year.

I was informed by Tony's cardiologist that he had interviewed a patient who had overcome these formidable odds. After receiving some quick CPR, the man who had passed out at the dinner table was revived. He told me he did not remember the incident. He had barely finished his dinner when he found himself on the floor, staring up at worried faces. "I have not felt any pain," he said. Don't be afraid. No feeling of a conclusion.

I wish this is how Tony's warm morning on Northampton Street may have gone.

Flinders Island

Since I got here, I haven't left Leeka. You can always find something new to observe. The weather changes, the wallabies' choreography, the constantly shifting light, and the Cape Barren geese's inquisitive looks.

But I have to go for a walk today. I suddenly feel the need to hike vigorously and stretch my body. Rock hopping to the north or south of here isn't appropriate. It's too remote, and I have to be careful not to trip on the slick stones. I wish there was more careless movement.

We'll have to endure the bumps, and I'm sorry for the car. We make our way through fragrant woodlands on the road out, moaning and squeaking. The aroma of eucalyptus is overwhelming, and the ti trees are in blossom. From one branch to another, green rosellas swoop.

The two must-do activities on the island, according to the guidebooks, are walking Trousers Point beach and climbing Mount Strzelecki. Strzelecki is an all-day hike, and unless I have to go to the other side, I have never enjoyed walking straight up mountains. Summits don't matter to me. Why should you labor to reach a windy summit just to obtain a wonderful view when there are so many other options? I therefore take a car to Trousers Point, the beach at the mountain range's western base, where the trailhead is located.

It really is amazing. With its expansive expanse of sand, immaculate dunes, crystal-clear waters, and a striking, jagged mountain backdrop, this beach is likely the most beautiful I have ever seen. Even more amazing than Big Sur is the contrast between land and water.

However, the pleasant barbeque facilities, the stone steps leading to the beach, and the presence of two other people while I'm there all cause me unreasonable annoyance. In Eden, I've been alone. I'd like to return there.

I had no idea how I would feel. Although I hadn't been scared to be alone, I didn't realize how much I would enjoy it. It feels more and more like an addiction now. I crave the complete peace and quiet of an empty landscape.

Then I realize I have not been alone. Being with Tony is allowing me to savor this moment. I can now think about him without being distracted in this loneliness. I may converse with his thoughts and read his journals. I can even discover new things about him, something I thought his passing had prevented me from doing.

No children, no pets, no editors, no publicists, no friends, no neighbors. Nobody is coming in on us here, no matter how much they love us. I can spend my entire conscious day by his side, and even into my unconscious nights.

This space has been created for him by solitude.

August 16, 2019
West Tisbury

The day eventually came for Tony's first memorial service, which I had planned on Martha's Vineyard. In Washington, D.C., Josh would be in charge of the following. As the two gatherings developed, it became apparent that the focus of the first would be Tony's adult life as a writer, historian, husband, and parent. The latter would go back in time and concentrate more on his early years, portraying him as the adored brother, uncle, and student in his boyhood family. Josh and I once again recognized the depth and diversity of Tony's friendships, and the richness of experiences he had accumulated over the years, as we organized the planning and divided up possible speakers according to who could be there in August or October.

I was unable to make any decisions at the moment, so I had picked the Vineyard date at random. If I had been rational, I would have known that it was the worst day of the year—the hottest day of the summer, when all the seats on the planes, the ferries, and the rooms on the Vineyard had been reserved months in advance.

I had burdened both myself and our friends. I had spent weeks trying to figure out how to make acquaintances here and hide them with islanders—a couch here, a guesthouse there. People had generously offered up these areas. There was a part of me that knew it would all work. The other half was always agitated: Would everyone be alright? A memorial is like a gloomy wedding, when everyone on the planet is invited, and you have no idea how many of the countless potential guests will actually show up. There is a tremendous pressure to do it correctly—to honor life. Another thing a grieving person is not willing to accomplish is this.

The Old Whaling Church in Edgartown, which was constructed by shipwrights in 1843, was a historic structure that Tony adored. The interior is flooded with light from the large, mullioned windows of this Greek Revival building. I hurried around that morning collecting flowers, setting up carpools for visitors from out of town, and setting up glasses of water for the eulogists. I changed into a black dress and sat down in the front pew, which is the wretched seat that most of us will eventually occupy. Dressed handsomely in a blue blazer and Tony's favorite tie, Bizu plucked up the bravery to serve as emcee, sincerely welcoming and thanking those who had traveled and those who had provided assistance.

Most of the friends of authors are themselves writers, and the eulogies were well-written, heartfelt, and humorous, capturing Tony's personality and achievements.

Martha, who married on our Waterford porch, talked about how difficult it was to come to terms with Tony's absence. She remarked, "Tony seems more here than a lot of people who actually are." Tony brightened every space he entered. He should be dead, but he's lighting this one, I mean.

During our years in London, our next-door neighbor Michael ridiculed Tony's habit of placing bets with friends, saying, "He probably owes everyone in this room dinner or a bottle of wine." He noted that Tony's writing career was also a string of wagers: wagers he made on strangers and wagers they made on him, allowing him access to their lives and sharing their experiences with him. "Tony went around disarming people in a world where there were many weapons."

In his late twenties, my nephew Sam had spent a year living with us. "To Sam, a pathetic excuse for a man," Tony wrote in Sam's copy of Confederates in the Attic, perhaps encapsulating the tight friendship he and Tony had developed. Tony, with love.

Sam was requested to perform "Forever Young" by Bob Dylan. Instead of starting the song, he paused and grinned longingly after adjusting the microphone and strumming the opening few chords. Tony would undoubtedly find a way to cruelly make fun of me for what is to come. However, here we go.

Last to speak was Nathaniel. He had grown up in a fantasy realm, which he referred to as his Wizarding realm, and I felt more at ease accompanying him there than Tony did. Fat fantasy novels with elves and dragons were Natty's favorite books; I loved them, but Tony didn't. Natty moved more in my orbit than his father's, was depressed about sports, enthusiastic about his harp lessons, and constantly wrote and illustrated his own magical stories. That started to change when he was in his teens. Like his father, he was an enthusiastic and skilled chess player, joined the high school football team, and got engrossed in current affairs. Father and son interests began to coincide. The two went on a crazy college tour when Nathaniel was seventeen. It was the type of road trip that showed Tony at his best: he connected with people of all kinds, opened doors that should have remained closed, and traveled unlikely distances with a schedule that was always changing if a better opportunity arose. They came back together in a new, mature friendship.

What he would say in his eulogy was not anything we had discussed. He went to the podium, drank a glass of water, and paused to look around the audience. Then, without hesitation or notes, he spoke straight from the heart. He talked about the solace he found in the fact that Tony's death was unexpected and unexpected. He expressed his appreciation that he, Bizu, and I all remembered a pleasant last encounter with Tony. He then recounted how, in the immediate aftermath of Tony's passing, he found it hard to look at his father's books at the bookstore or around the house because he saw them as a faint reflection of the man he had lost. That changed as the weeks went by: "He was always at his sharpest, funniest, most philosophical, bravest, and most adventurous in his writing. You would laugh till you sobbed because of the excellent prose. I see now his books do not reflect him. They are the essence of his being, the epitome of what it means to be a good man and a great adventurer. Through those books on our reading chairs, handbags, bedside tables, and tubs—in our hearts, thoughts, and words—he is with us. When we decide to look for him, he's at his best. There is no greater consolation than that, considering the certainty of loss.

Josh was sobbing next to me as our rabbi stood up to say kaddish. I was unable to cry. I was exhausted and depleted. Gnarled, desirous.

Jimi Hendrix's razor-edged guitar shriek blasted the roof off that old structure as everyone stood to leave the seats after Bizu returned to the stage to invite everyone to a celebration.
"Are You Skilled?"
Tony's favorite song was this.

Flinders Island

I used to get severe fevers a lot when I was younger. My parents took me to specialists, and I had blood drawn all the time. They did not provide a definitive diagnosis, and I finally outgrew whatever it was. I used to writhe in my parents' bed while the fevers were raging, seeing the ceiling and walls swell and contract in surreal undulations. Eventually, something amazing would always occur. My temperature would abruptly go away, and I would wake up cool and pain-free after falling asleep sweating and aching. A breeze would blow over my face as the voile curtains rose. I could see the Christmas bush's crimson blossoms burning brightly against the azure sky through the window of my bedroom. It was so beautiful I could enjoy it again. I was aware of the value of that sense of wellbeing even as a young child. Until you don't have it, it seems so normal.

As the days pass in this serene life of recollected love, I believe something similar is occurring to me. The dreams, the loneliness, the days, and the nights. I start to sense the soul unclenching and unfolding. It's a delicate, tentative thing. I'm scared to question it. The anguish could return with the fever still unbroken if I test the notion that I might be easing into a state of happiness.

More work needs to be done.

August 20, 2019
West Tisbury

The out-of-towners left the island jointly and severally in the days after the commemoration.

On their way to the airport, some people, like Deborah, stopped in for a final visit. The only pair who had reported from the Middle East together, as we had, were she and her husband—he for television, she for radio. A few months prior, he had passed away gradually after a protracted illness. We picked at a fruit platter while sitting in the garden. She shared some advice she had received from Ruth Bader Ginsburg through a colleague.

"Get your task done. Even while it might not be your best work, it will still be good and will save your life. Deborah had heeded that counsel and returned to her work covering the suffering of Syrian refugees. I could see myself doing that—losing myself in the terrible suffering of others. Crawling back to my desk to complete the task of imagination was something I couldn't have imagined.

The last person to depart was my mother-in-law. Before she left for her flight back to Washington, DC, Ellie and I were going to have lunch at the small café at the airport. She said that Simba, our cuddly little rescue mutt, my mother's companion in her last years, the tiniest of our dogs but the leader of the home, was standing just in front of the car as I loaded her things into the trunk.

I said as I got into the driver's seat, "Don't worry." "Simba always moves to the side."

I moved forward. A thump. Our seventeen-year-old dog had remained still just this one time. I sat there for a moment, refusing to believe what had happened. What I had just done. I then threw myself onto the gravel after exiting the vehicle.

He was still alive. His large brown eyes were still trusting as he gazed up at me. I quickly hurried to the veterinarian after picking up his lifeless corpse and placing it on my lap. I failed to put the car in park as I hurried out of it in a panic, clutching his tender body to my heart. It continued rolling slowly into a tree stand. Glancing back to make sure Ellie was okay, I ran inside and called for the veterinarian. It wasn't good. Simba had died in the few minutes it took to get there. It had been crushed by my front wheel, as revealed by a dent in his small cranium.

I had never struck a living creature in my fifty years of driving. I had jammed on the brakes to dodge deer on the Vineyard and swerved around rabbits in the Outback. In case it was a creature, my sons reprimanded me for stopping short whenever a dead leaf flitted over the road. I had also slain my dog.

I sat with Ellie at the airport, hoping the minutes would go by and her airline would announce boarding. I tried not to show too much emotion so as not to put more strain on this week, suffering woman. After that, I returned home by myself and excavated a grave behind an old cedar tree.

I didn't want to know if 2019 has any more tragedies in store.

Flinders Island

Two wooden daybeds facing the sea are situated side by side on the porch of this cottage. I imagine Tony on the straw hat next to me, reading a book or napping, as I lie here on warm afternoons with my straw hat over my face. I act as though the quiet is simply the two of us conversing silently.

Being outside at night is even more enjoyable. The island's stars also put me in my place, as its rocks do. Nature serves as a merciless reminder of how inconsequential humans are. There is no escaping the fact that we are inconsequential, whether it is day or night.

Since my arrival on the island, the moon has diminished, and now the ocean is illuminated only by starlight in the darkness of a new moon. So many stars. Here, the Milky Way streaks are dense and white, dazzling against the velvety darkness, and the Pleiades are much more than seven sisters.

On summer evenings as a kid, I would scale our back veranda's corrugated iron roof, which was still warm from the afternoon sun. Lying on my back, I would keep an eye out for shooting stars. The thought of all galaxies spinning in endless darkness would make my brain itch. Compared to prior times, Sydney is today considerably larger, brighter, and more flamboyant. A child in one of those inner suburbs probably wouldn't see anything anymore. I'm reminded of those summer evenings by the abundance of these visible stars here.

"Before you left, you showed me the bravery of stars and how light endures forever, even after death." The lyrics are from Ryan O'Neal's song "Saturn," in which he plays Sleeping at Last. It is a song about a dying person sharing wisdom with a loved one who is still alive, about how it is a remarkable chance to have lived at all, a rare and wonderful coincidence to have lived and experienced consciousness.

To have flourished is even more amazing and uncommon in this broken, hurting world. to have discovered happiness, contentment, safety, and love.

We didn't talk on the deathbed. If Tony had been given the opportunity, I'll never know what advice he would have wanted to share.

I am aware that it is my responsibility to bear his light. To maintain him brightly lit for my boys and their offspring—his grandchildren—whenever they come to visit.

West Tisbury

I took Bizu back to school in my car shortly after the memorial service. I came home to find our surviving dog, our clumsy, affectionate Bear, alone in the house.

The September of 2019 Vineyard was the most gorgeous in ten years, but I couldn't tell if that was a sign of mercy or cruelty. Even when the first leaves started to flush and gild, the grass stayed stubbornly green since it had rained during the normally dry month of August.

I went from feeling grateful that this beauty was assisting me in rising and facing the day to feeling sad that Tony was not present to enjoy the changing leaves, the dim light, and the cricket and katydid sounds as the evening wore on. His favorite season was autumn.

September had been our summer until 2005, when we made the move to the Vineyard year-round. When the Vineyard's rentals dropped, we were able to find a dilapidated shack that we could afford to rent for a week or two, so that's when we went on vacation. Since he was a young boy, Tony had been visiting the island. Unexpectedly, when I was eleven years old in Sydney, I made a pen friend there named Joannie. I had corresponded with her throughout my adolescence and early twenties after meeting her through the Mr. Spock fan club. I had hoped to see her when I arrived in New York for graduate school, as I mentioned in Foreign Correspondence, but it was not to be: A few months before my arrival, Joannie passed away following a protracted battle with anorexia.

Before receiving the job offer from The Wall Street Journal, I had intended to return to Sydney as soon as I received my degree. I told Tony that before I left for home, I was determined to see the Vineyard, the only destination in America. He took me there over Labor Day weekend in 1983.

Later, Tony expressed his relief that my pen friend wasn't from a chilly nook of some ugly, blizzard-prone industrial town. He was aware that I would adore the Vineyard's rural community and natural beauty, and that the prospect of living there would add another arrow to his arsenal of arguments regarding the prospects for an American future.

Particularly during the years when they were our sole break from the relentless grind of covering wars abroad, those stolen weeks in September had been enchanted. We would read poetry, grill fish over driftwood fires, paint amateurish watercolors, and relax on the beach. What would it be like to live on the island all year round? We decided to find out in 2005 after both of us had given up journalism to write books. With children attending school and volunteering in the community, we adapted to island life.

But suddenly, despite all the beauty and the encouragement of devoted friends, I wished I was somewhere else. I had a strong desire to flee this vacant house and the barrage of memories it held.

Living in Boston, Nathaniel was deeply focused on his work, looking for novel treatments for the most difficult illnesses. Bizu had made the decision to travel to Ethiopia for winter break to spend December instructing children in English at a distant rural assistance facility. I was therefore not required to stay after the Thanksgiving holiday. I escaped to Sydney after finding a buddy to look after my dog and horse.

I reached the entrance of hell. The whole country was on fire, the sky were black with smoke, and the news was filled with unfamiliar terms like "ember attack," "finger of fire," "watch and wait," "too late to leave," "pyrocumulonimbus clouds," and "dry lightning that warned of danger." It was a season of mourning, a period of dread.

On December 31, after the worst of the fires had finally been contained, my sister and I stood in Balmain Park with a view of Sydney Harbor and said goodbye to the worst year ever.

2020, the new one, would need to be superior. That's what I thought.

I didn't feel much better. Tony and I had been happy in Sydney, therefore I was miserable there.

After more than a year of Midwest commutes, they were first newlyweds enjoying the luxury of living together. Walking Nathaniel to school later as parents. vivid moments when we were young and content, settling into our lives as writers and understanding that, against all the obstacles, this new job would succeed. Everywhere you looked, you could find recollections. I was oppressed by nostalgia, lamenting the charred bushland and the suffering of smoldering animals, and I was unable to find comfort in Sydney.

So I fled once more, to Paris, a place where Tony and I had no common ancestry. I lived in an apartment in the 1st arrondissement with antique beams and a view of roofs, and I had a writers' residency at the American Library next to the Eiffel Tower. The Paris grisaille reflected my February mood. Perhaps I would be able to resume writing in a different setting with different routines.

The walk from my apartment to the library took thirty minutes. Each day I took a different path, using a different bridge to cross the Seine. The visiting writer had his own office in the basement, a space without a view, a far cry from the picturesque panorama of trees and streams that surrounded my home study. As I unpacked my reference books and turned on my laptop, I reasoned that there wouldn't be much to divert my attention here.

The library director stopped by that day with some wipes and a bottle of antiseptic cleanser. She shrugged and placed them on my desk, saying, "They say there is a bad virus."

No one in Paris seemed to care if such were the case. Paris was in denial, but the news from Italy was alarming. Before leaving for lacrosse training camp in Florida, Bizu came to Paris to spend a week of his spring vacation with me. The full moon, a disk of light perched just on the apex of I. M. Pei's pyramid was a sight to behold as I returned home after dining with old friends from my reporting days in Kurdistan. I walked by eateries and cafés packed with Parisians.

In the street outside my apartment, gendarmes started building barricades two days later. There were no restaurants open. I heard Donald Trump declare he was closing America's borders late that evening. We might be stuck in my borrowed flat for an indeterminate amount of time, at the end of a line in a health system that I was unfamiliar with, if we did not depart right now. I packed my belongings into my suitcase and went to Charles de Gaulle Airport, where I sat on the floor using my laptop to book flight after flight and then watch as each was canceled. I was able to secure seats on a plane bound for Atlanta that was scheduled to depart in an hour. I took hold of them. It's difficult to remember how little any of us knew about what was about to happen at the time. No one wore masks or realized at the time that they were protective, so we fumbled for gloves and antiseptic wipes for the flight.

Nathaniel was home already. He had installed two PCs in Tony's office in the barn and was working quickly because the biotech industry was booming and this virus needed to be stopped. Bizu's boarding school had closed, his spring training trip had been postponed, and his lacrosse season had been canceled. I was glad we weren't stranded on different continents and could be together. We hunkered down, thinking how Tony would have responded to lockdown and how his outgoing nature would have been restrained in such a constrained environment. Therefore, we were unaware that this pandemic would persist into the spring and summer, with masks, social separation, case spikes, and concern that persisted into the New Year. We saw live coverage of men assaulting the Capitol on January 6, 2021, while flying rebel flags. I thought Tony would be there with his notebook. Long before anybody else paid attention, he had sought out and interviewed those white supremacists and neo-Confederates, constantly trying to figure out how and why they had come to hold such beliefs. His topic had been the great American divide: rich-poor, urban-rural, North-South. I assumed that at least a dozen of the guys who were thronging those marble halls had shared a beer with him. He was supposed to cover the story, so I was disappointed that he was unable to.

I was happy to have my boys home and to have some unplanned extra time to spend as a mother. I'm glad it's quiet. And I was relieved that I no longer had to act like everything was normal. For everyone, nothing was normal. There was grief everywhere.

I dived into cooking as dining out was out of the question. I began recording the number of dinners I could prepare before repeating a recipe. (I reached number 48.) I took long walks and befriended two calves on a neighbor's farm. They met me and ran to the stone wall when they spotted me. Their liquid brown eyes begged for pats and tickles, making it impossible for me to ever eat beef again.

I made my way back to my desk, finished the novel, and dedicated it to Tony in this forced, strangely calm life.

Flinders Island

I've developed new routines that are unique to this area as the weeks have gone by. Every afternoon, I go for a lengthy swim to signal the change from afternoon to evening. At that time, the tide is at its highest, the wind has slowed, and the weather is typically at its most stable.

I deviated from that regimen today and went for a late walk. I return hungry and miss the swim. I feel bad about my decision as the sun sets. Despite the waning light, I make my way to the shore, strip off, and jump in.

Though not chilly, the water feels crisp across my skin. It's so clear that I can see the chips in my five-week-old pedicure as I tread water. The clouds are tinted shades of gold and yellow as the sun sets.

I fell under the surf. It has a mikveh-like feel. I descend, far from all the memories I've evoked over the previous few weeks. All of that period's commotion, suffering, and foolishness. I allowed everything to be carried away by the waves' pull. I rise and confront the vastness of the ocean.

I let the music develop and unfold like a fern. I let my lungs out as I howl.

It's a startling sound, raw and loud in this still world. I let myself drop once again before rising to confront the sky's fiery hues. The sun's descent appears to signal a more certain conclusion than just a day. Any day could be the last day, including today. Everyone is aware of that. I sense it now.

With another howl, I lift its weight and launch it back into the air. Once more down, then east, where the first light appeared. Tony will never see that light again. For the life he no longer has and the life we no longer have together, I cry out for him.

There's nothing left when I head back toward the shack. Finally, I'm exhausted. The only thing left is a long, drawn-out sigh.

I read some guidance on the craft of novel writing when I first started writing fiction. Throughout the story, it is your responsibility as an author to keep your protagonist's head underwater. At the end, though, you have to choose between sinking them or letting them swim.
I submerged my face in the brackish, clear water. I extend my body. I go swimming.

Afterword

Nice conclusion, huh?
It's not the end. Not the end of Tony's sorrow. That will continue.
I'm aware that things will occasionally grow worse. when one of them becomes a father, when Bizu completes college, and when Nathaniel is the bridegroom. It's conceivable that they will wed someone who has never met Tony and won't have any memories of him to share with his grandchildren. I will be saddened by this. And I will miss Tony as a grandfather—the humorous Zaydeh who pushed his grandchildren to do outrageous things. Zaydeh, who was loved by his grandchildren. Not the end of mourning, then. Not even the conclusion of my hut stay. There, I spent more days there. I visited the Mother Rock, wrote, read Tony's writings, swam, and offered up whatever resembled prayer for someone who didn't have a recipient address. I discovered a spot on the beach that resembled a thoughtfully designed rock garden. Cool green euphorbias and vibrant purple ice plant blooms dotted the cracks between the heaved-up stones and the scouring salt. Life, working hard.
With only wallabies, pademelons, and finally a lone, waddling wombat for company, I relished the isolation. I saved the silence before going back to the world of noise.
Indeed, I think I could have had a nice existence on Flinders Island if I hadn't met Tony: a flannel-clad, wind-burned writer and gardener who volunteered at the small school and with environmental organizations while grumpily fighting unsuitable expansion. It is impossible to know who would have supported me in that alternate existence or whether or not we would have produced children together. So I tossed such conjectures to the windy winds. I make the decision to cherish the life I've lived in this unique and lovely location, surrounded by affection.
I had to write this because I had to. Reliving the tragedy of the death by going back to the moments repeatedly and making an effort to

remember more details each time is one way to treat "complicated grief." I have attempted to achieve that.

Yiyun Li, a novelist, describes the dilemma of writing about an unexpected death. The more you remember, the more elusive that death becomes. That hasn't been true for me. I've gone to a place where I can experience Tony's death, slowing it down, absorbing it, and going through the pain I needed to.

Some situations are difficult to remember, and some memories are illusive. I can't recall the exact words I used to inform Bizu about his father's passing. That memory has been erased by the darkness that enveloped me when I heard him weep. Nathaniel and I had a hazy first discussion as well. I just recall the startle of knowing that he already knew—that someone else's words had reached him more quickly than mine had.

One of my closest friends, a widower, was among the first to insist on seeing me the day after I returned from Washington, D.C. He stated he could not wait to give me the three most important things he learned from his personal loss. He said, "Make it safe for people to talk about Tony." He had been hurt and angry when no one had brought up his beloved wife, Gretchen, the first time he had gone out after her death. He understood that for others to talk about her, he had to first. I still abide by this great suggestion and bring Tony along for every discussion.

"Don't return home to a quiet house," he advised. Don't turn off the radio. I told him I didn't think it would be an issue for me because I had two dogs at the time, both of whom were eager greeters.

However, what was his third statement?

I know I followed the advice, and I know it was sound. It's gone now, buried in my jumbled recollections of those early days, whatever it was. The capital city of Benin and the third decimal position for pi are undoubtedly lost.

Now that I'm back in the spotlight and the noisy rhythms of my actual, frequently public life, I can start evaluating the effectiveness of this self-administered therapy. Immediately, I realized that, as nature always does, spending time alone in nature healed me. "I know the suffering exists beside wet grass and a bright blue sky recently scrubbed by rain," says Ann Patchett's protagonist in her book Tom Lake. Anxiety and beauty are equally real.

I now devote more time to beauty at home. I always take the time to observe the trees in all their seasonal variations. Spend time with the creatures that occupy my space. More than almost anything else, seeing a nest of baby bunnies, a coin-sized painted turtle hatchling, or a fluffy mallard duckling swimming for the first time will lift my spirits.

And I've noticed something else. I was able to place one of the bundles in the luggage of my grief during my stay on Flinders Island. It's the sorrow I had been harboring for the life I had anticipated and the life I would have lived. It was life with the rocking chairs facing the sunset, growing old with Tony at my side, laughing, debating the news, reliving old memories, and feeling proud of our sons as they boldly entered adulthood. There is nothing that can restore that life. I've come to terms with that. I have set out to make my life as meaningful and vibrant as possible. "Get to work," Bader Ginsburg urged. That is what I do, then.

I have a modest and subtle goal for what I have said here. I wish certain things could be different. I doubt that our contemporary, secular society can devise a more compassionate approach to grieving. We might be able to accommodate something like "Sorry Business," "iddah," "sheloshim," or "chehelom," but I'm not sure.

I simply hope that the bereaved have some time and space, no matter how short or long, to be melancholy—what Victor Hugo called the happiness of sadness.

Our culture dislikes sadness. We want everyone to be content. When they're not, we're chagrined and a little offended. The intention is to lift their spirits. Later, if their mourning is thought to last too long, they will gaze at their wristwatch and tap their foot if they are unable to be encouraged. I hope we are able to withstand those things.

Additionally, I hope that the U.S. medical-forensic establishment will reconsider its cruel methods and create better procedures for handling loved ones' remains and their mourners in the first few hours after death.

Journalist Leigh Sales examines what happens to people when pain and loss abruptly upend their lives in her book Any Ordinary Day. All the cases she records are well-known disasters in Australia. To deliver the news to the next of kin, police and occasionally religious leaders show up in person in each of them. Nobody picks up the phone and blabbers it out. Sales cites the example of Matt Richell, a young publisher who was killed in a surfing accident after being thrown against rocks. Hannah, his wife, went to the morgue to see his body, and a woman there gave her a detailed account of what she would see, including the room's layout, the clothes he was wearing, the color of the sheet covering him, and the appearance of the wounds on his head and face. She informed Hannah that she was free to enter by herself or with a companion and to remain for whatever long she desired.

It's odd to say that you're envious of someone else's visit to a morgue, but when I read that story, I felt jealous of Hannah. Really, how difficult might it be to give the grieving this meager token of humanity? A little empathy. The request is not excessive.

However, it is difficult to alter institutional practices. Therefore, I offer a suggestion that anyone can follow on their own—a straightforward routine for long-term couples. Write down every chore you don't want to talk about that keeps the house running well, the set of balancing torches that only you know how to wield. Up until the day they never anticipated, all the minor details your partner didn't think they would need to know.

I have little doubt that Tony would not have known where to locate the water stop valve in the event of a pipe rupture, or even the name of the plumber to call to fix it, if I had passed away unexpectedly. He most likely would have had trouble locating the children's immunization records or the login credentials for their report cards. Like so many other items in his job basket, those were in mine.

Everyone should create a document, in my opinion. Update it from time to time and call it Your Life: How It Works. I would have had more time to devote to the essential grief process and less time to time-consuming material activities if I had such a document.

Finally, share your tale in whatever way that suits you.

Put it in writing, discuss it with a therapist, and tell your friends about it. Take charge of this pivotal point in your life's story. Salman Rushdie came out to speak at Columbia University while still hiding following Ayatollah Khomeini's fatwa. "Those who lack the ability to retell, rethink, deconstruct, joke about, and alter the story that governs their lives as circumstances change are genuinely helpless," he stated. This dying story is the one that takes up most of my time. I've retold and rethought it here. I can't alter it, though. Tony has passed away. The present tense. For as long as I live, he will be dead, right here, in my present. I can't alter that narrative. The only thing I can alter is myself.

"Write what you know to be true," urged Old Man Hemingway.

Here it is, dear reader.